The
INTERNET GUIDE
for PSYCHOLOGY

The
INTERNET GUIDE
for PSYCHOLOGY

David Mahony
St. John's University

HOUGHTON MIFFLIN COMPANY   BOSTON   TORONTO

Geneva, Illinois   Palo Alto   Princeton, New Jersey

Senior Associate Editor: Jane Knetzger
Editorial Assistant: Gwyneth V. Fairweather
Project Editor: Helen Bronk
Senior Manufacturing Coordinator: Priscilla Bailey

Printed in the U.S.A.

ISBN: 0-395-78566-9

123456789-B-00 99 98 97 96

CONTENTS

INTRODUCTION

What Is the Internet?

During the 1960s, the U.S. Defense Department's Advanced Research Projects Agency (ARPA) began to conduct research to see if computers in different locations could communicate and share data with one another. They wanted to design a system that could survive a nuclear war so that if one computer was destroyed the other computers could still communicate with one another. They developed a system known as ARPANET. This system allowed computers to send data back and forth to one another, and more important, it allowed researchers to send electronic messages (*e-mail*) to one another.

As ARPANET grew, some enterprising college students developed a way to connect their school's computers to it and hold on-line conferences. In this way, people from all over the world could converse with one another using computers. The system grew in leaps and bounds, and by the 1980s this network of computers became known as the *Internet* (from "Internet-working"). Soon, colleges, research companies, and government agencies began to connect their computers to the Internet. By the 1990s, private companies such as America Online™, Prodigy™, and Compuserve™ began to connect their computers to the Internet and offer Internet access to individuals for a fee. What has resulted is a network of millions of computers, all over the world, that are connected to one another by phone lines and accessible by almost everyone.

In order to use the Internet, you need an *Internet application program*. These programs, of which there are many different types, allow you to access the information on the Internet. This guide is designed so that each chapter gives you information about each Internet application program. E-mail (electronic mail), the most popular Internet application program, allows you to send messages to anyone, anywhere in the world, as long as they too have an e-mail account. Group discussions are often held using e-mail so that people all over the world can discuss a topic with one another. Electronic bulletin boards are also very popular Internet application programs. Just like regular bulletin boards, these are places where you can read and post messages. Thousands of bulletin boards, known collectively as *Usenet*, are on the Internet. Each bulletin board has its own special topic of discussion and can include pictures, video clips, and sound clips.

The later developments on the Internet are the programs that will search for and display information that you are interested in. *Gopher* (because it "goes for" the information) was one of the first applications designed to search out and retrieve information for you. One of the latest Internet access programs, the *World Wide Web* (or *WWW* or the *Web*) allows you to view text or pictures and even to hear sounds on just about any type of information that interests you. These programs, along with the computers all over the world that are connected to one another, are collectively known as the Internet.

In addition, *FTP sites* are places on the Internet where software can be *downloaded*. Downloading means to copy a computer file from a computer on the Internet to your computer. These sites can be accessed with *FTP programs*.

Recently, many commercial companies have been providing individuals with access to the Internet. Companies like America Online™, Prodigy™, and Compuserve™ offer connections to the Internet for a fee. You can access the information that they keep on their own computers or connect to the Internet through them. These companies also have their own electronic bulletin boards and e-mail systems.

What Can Be Done on the Internet?

There is no end to what can be done on the Internet. This guide will show you how the Internet can be used to access psychological information, communicate with others in the field of psychology, stay up to date with the latest information, and express your own opinion on psychological theories and research. Designed to help those of you who are new to the Internet access information, this guide will not make traditional searches for information in libraries obsolete, but it will show you additional research sources that are available and demonstrate alternative ways to conduct traditional searches. Information that is available through your local library can be supplemented and may soon be available on the Internet.

There are many advantages to retrieving information on the Internet—mainly, the information is current and up to date. Traditional library searches will give you information that is at least one year old. This is because most scientific journal articles take a year or so to become published. It also takes time to incorporate the *abstracts* onto *databases* such as *PsycLit*™. Overall, when an article is included in an abstract database, the research itself may already be two or three years old. In comparison, the research and information that you access on the Internet can be as little as one or two weeks old. In addition, the information on the Internet is interactive. If someone posts research results that you disagree with or find some flaws in, you can communicate with that person instantly. Psychological theories and practices are always debated on the Internet, and you can contribute to these debates no matter what your title or degree is as long as your opinions are relevant.

Research   There are many ways to search for research findings on the Internet. You can search your own university library or other libraries through the Internet. There are *on-line journals* that publish results of research recently conducted. You can even publish your own research results in these journals. Most important, there are many nontraditional sources of information for research purposes. You can learn about new psychopharmacological drug treatments that are available before any published studies come out. You can communicate with individuals that suffer from psychological disorders and get information on what it's like to live with a psychological disorder that is not available through traditional methods. You can listen in and contribute to support groups for people that suffer from all kinds of addiction problems, including substance and sexual abuse. You can access the latest psychological theories and find out about their shortcomings and future directions before it is published in any journal.

Something to keep in mind is that traditional journals submit their articles to other experts in the field to critique the research and make sure that it is accurate. Research that is available on the Internet is not always *peer reviewed* (reviewed by peers for accuracy). Non-peer-reviewed research may not be valid or accurate. Whenever you reference research that you find on the Internet, you should be aware of its peer-review status.

Library Searches   Library searches are also available on the Internet. You can search the card catalogues of your university or any other library as long as it is connected to the Internet. Many libraries have limited resources, so before you go to your local libraries, you can search their card catalogues to determine whether or not they have the information that you're interested in.

Discussions with Psychology Professionals   Another important resource on the Internet is access to discussions held by the researchers in any given field. Discussion groups exist where you can listen in to the latest theories and practices that are used by psychologists in every area of psychology. In this manner, you can find out what the latest work being done is in any given area and ask questions and contribute to these discussions.

Software   Software can be downloaded over the Internet. Many software packages for psychological report writing as well as many statistical programs are available—some for no charge. Assessment scales are also available that can be used to determine a person's score on many types of psychological variables.

Latest Information   Information on the Internet is state of the art. There are no delays to information published on the Internet and no restrictions on who presents the information. The Internet will give you access to information that has not yet been published in traditional journals or books.

Exchange of Ideas   Ideas can be exchanged on the Internet. Let's say that you have some concerns regarding a certain psychological theory. You can present your concerns and discuss them with the leading researchers in the field. You can even offer feedback to others that are having discussions on the Internet. In this forum, the information you know is more important than the degree or status you have. If you disagree with a long-standing psychological theory and want to write a paper on it and send it to others, you can.

Graduate School and Employment Notices   The Internet is an excellent place to network. It is a unique way to communicate and network with psychologists all over the world. There are discussions about the pros and cons of various graduate schools, internships, and postdoctorate positions. If you are interested in applying to a certain graduate school, you can post e-mail stating this, and you will receive valuable information from that school's students and faculty about requirements for acceptance and a critical review of the school's training.

Job opportunities all over the world are posted on the Internet, as are internship and postdoctorate positions. You can contact individuals in these positions and get information from them on the best way to find out about a certain job or internship.

This Guide

This guide was written especially for students that have some knowledge of computers but are unfamiliar with the Internet. Each chapter follows a step-by-step approach and goes over a particular Internet program. Also included is a list of valid, universal commands for each particular Internet program. Since thousands of different Internet programs are out there, all the commands could not possibly be covered in this manual. What is included is the name of the command that you will need to know and some universal commands that may work on some systems. Most Internet programs will have a *menu*, or *menu system*, with all the commands listed; if not, you will have to find out how to run the commands from your local computer center.

In this manual, a standard syntax is used to translate the commands to the reader. For example, while entering commands into your computer, you may have to press the Enter key or include personal information such as your name. The following table shows the syntax used in this guide for Internet commands. This syntax is commonly used on the Internet itself.

For example, if the guide says:

To access the Internet, type "**open {your full name}**" <enter>

You would type:

open David Mahony

and then you would press the Enter key.

COMMAND SYNTAX

\<ENTER\> OR \<RETURN\>	PRESS THE ENTER KEY.
Quotation marks, e.g., "**help**"	Any command that is typed in bold and surrounded by quotation marks should be typed in exactly as it appears, but *do not* type in the quotation marks. They are there only to show you where the command begins and ends.
Braces	Commands surrounded by braces, e.g., {your name}, will be information that you have to type in. When you type the command, *do not* include the braces.
Spaces, periods, commas, etc.	Spaces, periods, commas, asterisks, or other characters should by typed in exactly as they appear.

Although the Internet can be chaotic and confusing, it is a fun place. The step-by-step instructions in this guide, along with information from your local computer center, will familiarize you with some of the basics of the Internet. Keep in mind that the Internet is a place where you can explore any interests that you have and meet people from all over the world. You do not have to limit yourself to psychology. Do what you enjoy most on the Internet, and you will learn to get around the Internet in no time.

CHAPTER 1: INTERNET ACCESS

Getting an Internet Account

Getting an Internet account should be as easy as contacting your classroom instructor or your university computer center and informing them that you would like an account. You may already have an account that you use to send e-mail to friends. Once you have an account, the first thing to do is to find out who the *systems operator* (sysop) is and what his or her *e-mail address* is. Your local sysop will be the one that you contact when you need help with your Internet access system. The sysop is the person that runs your system, so he or she will be the person that can answer your questions. It is preferable to communicate with the sysop through e-mail since he or she may spend a great deal of time on the Internet and may prefer this type of communication. If your sysop is not available to answer your questions, find out who is or get the appropriate documents from your computer center.

Your sysop will provide you with an *Internet access account*, a *password*, as well as *logon* and introductory instructions for your Internet account. If you have a *modem* (a device that will connect your computer to a phone line) and wish to connect to the Internet from your own personal computer at home, your sysop will provide you with the necessary *communications software* and the information necessary to set it up. Otherwise, you can usually access your account at your local computer center.

If your school does not offer Internet access, commercial providers such as Compuserv™, Prodigy™, or America Online™ will offer you Internet access from your home for an hourly fee. Their phone numbers should be available in your local yellow pages or in computer magazines.

To get started, you will need to know your *logon procedure* and password. If you are logging on from home, you will need the appropriate communications software and the correct telephone number(s). Give yourself some time to accustom yourself to the Internet. If you are a new *user*, you may want to logon and *surf* around before you continue with this guide. Surfing is a term that means to look around, browse through the *menus*, and try out the various services that your local provider offers you.

You will be provided with a password, but you should change your password every three months or so. There are individuals on the Internet, known as *hackers*, that specialize in obtaining access to others' accounts by gaining access to their password. When you create your password, do not use words that are in English or foreign language dictionaries. Use a combination of letters and numbers in your password, and change it every three months or so. This will ensure that your account is not easily broken into.

6

If your account is broken into, hackers can use it for all sorts of devious activities, including breaking into other computer systems, stealing software, and other illegal activities. If they do this from your account, it will appear as though you are the one that is doing it. If you suspect that your account has been broken into, contact your local sysop and change your password immediately.

Keep in mind that all Internet access accounts are different. Some offer more than others. Most accounts will offer e-mail, File Transfer Protocol, Gopher, and access to the World Wide Web. If yours does not, there are always ways to access them although this manual is not designed to demonstrate alternative ways to gain access to various Internet *sites*.

Helpful Commands and Terms

Before you get started on the Internet, you should be aware of several things. No matter where you are on the Internet, if you are stuck, you can simply type "**help**" to receive instructions on how to navigate from where you are. Most Internet applications will respond to "**help**" with a list of valid commands to help you get to where you want to go.

There will also be a *cancel command*. This command will allow you to disconnect from the Internet in case you get stuck and can find no other way out. Sometimes, your screen will *freeze*. This means that you can type on the keyboard but nothing happens on the screen. If this happens, use the cancel command. Cancel commands are different for each system, so you will have to find out which one works on your system.

While you surf the Internet, you will find that on many occasions a site that is referred to in this guide, or elsewhere, no longer exists. Or you will run into dead ends and get error messages. Sometimes you won't be able to logon or will get disconnected while on the Internet. All these problems are unavoidable. The Internet consists of a bunch of computers that are connected by phone lines all over the world. Phone lines can go down, there may be power outages, computers go *down*, and sometimes Internet sites just disappear forever. If you have problems reaching an Internet site, check the *address* and try again. If you still can't reach it, try again in 24 hours. You will usually be able to access a site if you keep trying, but if you can't, it may no longer exist, and you will have to look elsewhere for the information that you want.

Privacy and Viruses

There is no guarantee that the activity that you conduct on the Internet will be private. E-mail that you send or receive on the Internet can be intercepted and read by others, so please be careful. Many companies are now developing programs that will ensure privacy on the Internet. Until then, assume that anything you do on the Internet can be seen by others.

In addition, there has been a great deal of publicity in the media about computer viruses on the Internet. Computer viruses are computer programs that can copy themselves onto your *floppy disks* or *hard drive*. For example, if you use a floppy disk in a computer at school and then insert it into your computer at home, you may inadvertently give a virus to your home computer. Once the viruses are there, they have the potential of destroying all of your computer files. To protect against this, you should install a *virus protection program* that will scan your disks for viruses and update the program regularly. Scan your disks every time you insert them into a computer other than your own. Virus protection programs may be available at your university computer center. The only way that you can get a virus from the Internet is if you download a software program and neglect to scan it for viruses.

Internet Activities

1. Contact your local sysop to establish an Internet access account.

2. Learn your logon procedure, including your password.

3. Surf around until you are comfortable with the logon procedure and the menu system or some of the commands for your Internet access account.

4. Learn how to change your password, and change it every three months.

5. Obtain a virus protection program from your local software distributor or from your local computer center.

CHAPTER 2: ELECTRONIC MAIL

Sending E-Mail

E-mail, or electronic mail, is the most powerful tool that you have access to on the Internet. Fortunately, every Internet account has e-mail access. E-mail is a form of communication that combines the speed of a telephone call with the detail and intimacy of a letter. Using your e-mail account, you can send letters to anyone in the world for free, as long as they also have an e-mail account. E-mail also offers convenience. Unlike telephone calls that need both people on the phone at the same time, e-mail can be sent and read at the user's convenience. Most users will check their e-mail once a day, so responses normally happen within 24 hours.

E-mail communication is fast, cheap, and comprehensive. E-mail can be saved, downloaded and printed out, responded to with the original message included, or forwarded to other interested users with your comments included.

In order to use your e-mail account, you will need to know several commands:

1. The first command you will need to know is how to open your mail program. After you logon to your system, find out the command to get into your e-mail program. Remember, there are too many different e-mail programs out there to include every possible command in this manual. Your system may have an easy-to-use menu system, or you may have to contact your sysop to find out the command.

2. Once you are in your mail program, you will see a menu with options, including those to send mail and read mail. Go to the send mail option.

3. Now you should see an *address field*. This is a blank space where you type in the e-mail address of the person you want to send your message to. You will need to know the person's e-mail address that you are writing to.

4. Type the address in the address field. Exchange e-mail addresses with someone in your class or a friend, and practice sending e-mail back and forth. Or, if you prefer, you can send e-mail to yourself. Here is an example of what an e-mail address looks like:

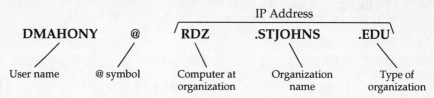

This is my e-mail address. Feel free to send me an e-mail to practice sending e-mail or to ask me a question that may come up while you read this guide.

Parts of an E-Mail Address

Every e-mail address has three parts: a user name, an @ symbol, and the address of the user's *mail server*. In the preceding example, the user name is DMAHONY (David Mahony), and the mail server is RDZ.STJOHNS.EDU (the RDZ computer at St. John's University). The mail server address is also called the *IP* (Internet Protocol) *address* or *domain name*. Each mail server connected to the Internet has an IP address. These addresses can be either in numerical form or, as you see in the example, in letter form. The letter form is usually used because it is easier to remember.

You can get a lot of information about an individual from his or her e-mail address. The first part of the address is usually an anagram of the user's name. In the example, DMAHONY is the user's name for my account. My full name is David Mahony. On some systems, the user does not pick his or her user name, and sometimes the user name is written in numbers. On these addresses, you may not be able to tell much about the user's real name.

The rest of the address is called the IP address. The best way to read the IP address is from right to left. The last three letters in an address will give you information about what type of organization the individual is associated with. In the example, my address says EDU. This means that I am writing from an educational institution. Since universities were one of the first institutions to offer Internet access to the public, many addresses will have an EDU at the end. Other institutions have the following suffixes:

.EDU   Educational site or university in the United States
.COM   Commercial site in the United States
.GOV   U.S. government site
.MIL   U.S. military site
.FR   Site in France
.CA   Site in Canada

There are many more examples, but these are some of the more commonly used suffixes. The next part, reading from right to left, is the name of the institution. Sometimes it will be obvious, such as my address, STJOHNS (St. John's University). Other times it may not be so easy to decipher because the institution's name is too long and has to be abbreviated. For example, the IP address for the University of Alabama is UA.EDU. You can see that this is an educational institution and that UA stands for the University of Alabama, but you may not know this if you were not told.

The last part of the IP address is the name of the computer or server that the user is using. In my address, I use the RDZ computer at St. John's University.

Here is another example:

CLINTON@WHITEHOUSE.GOV

Reading from right to left, we see that this address is from someone in the U.S. government (GOV) who uses a computer at the White House and goes by the name of Clinton. Guess who? You can even write him an e-mail if you want—that's his real address.

Once you know the e-mail address of the person that you want to write to, type it into the address field in your mail program. Again, since dozens of mail programs are available, there are too many commands and fields for me to cover them all here. If your e-mail program is not self-explanatory, contact your sysop or your computer center.

It should not matter whether you write the address in capital letters or in a mixture of small and capital letters, but you must spell the address correctly. If you don't have the proper address—if you misspell it or forget to include a period or @ symbol—your e-mail won't go through. If this happens, you will get an e-mail from *mailer-daemon*. Mailer-daemon is like the Internet post office telling you that your e-mail was undeliverable. The mailer-daemon e-mail will tell you that there was no user by that name or no IP address by that name. Keep in mind that the Internet is chaotic and quirky. Sometimes computers go down. If you send someone an e-mail and it is returned and you know that the address is correct, most likely his or her computer is down. If this happens, try again in 24 hours.

E-Mail Subject Lines

The next part to sending e-mail is the *subject line*, which is what the person you are sending the e-mail to will see on his or her e-mail program when your e-mail arrives. Your subject line should be one or two words that accurately describes the contents of your e-mail. For example, if you are requesting references from someone, your subject line should say something like REFERENCE REQUEST. If you are writing someone about a job, your subject line should say something like EMPLOYMENT INFO. The reason the subject line is used is that some users will receive many e-mails and cannot always read them all. When you open your e-mail program and go into your *inbox* or *mail received folder*, you will see a list of e-mails that you have received. You will see the user's name of the individual that sent the e-mail, the size of the e-mail in *bytes* (bytes are the way computer files are measured—the more bytes, the bigger the file or letter), and the subject line. Since some e-mail users receive several hundred e-mails a week, they read through the subject lines and read only the e-mails that interest them, deleting the others. So, include a clear, concise subject line on your e-mail. Most e-mail sent by an individual user will be read and responded to.

The next part of an e-mail is the body of the letter. This is where you write what you want to say to the person. Your mail program should work something like a word processor. You can add and delete lines and use a spell checker. Mail programs are not nearly as sophisticated as current word processors, so you will have to learn the commands that your mail program has. Usually, these commands are listed at the bottom or top of your screen. If the commands are not on the screen or if you have trouble editing e-mail, try to find the help function or contact your sysop. Remember, sysops prefer to be contacted via e-mail, so it would be a good idea to get your sysop's e-mail address.

Internet Activity

1. Send an e-mail to a friend or classmate (or to yourself). You do not have to write a long or detailed e-mail but just enough to see if you understand the commands.

CHAPTER 3: PROCESSING E-MAIL

Saving and Printing E-Mail

Once you learn how to read and send e-mail, there are some other options that you will need to know, for example, how to save, print, download, delete, reply to, and forward e-mail. Saving e-mail is usually easy: just don't delete it, and it will remain in your inbox. But beware, some e-mail accounts will delete e-mail that is left there for too long. If you want to print it out, there should be a command somewhere on your screen to do this. Some systems will let you print out an e-mail directly from the inbox. If you use the print command, the e-mail will usually print out at your local computer center. Sometimes you will have to tell the program what printer you want to print it out on. You will have to get this information from your sysop. If you don't have an option to print directly from the mail program or if you are using a modem from home, you will have to download the e-mail in order to print it out.

Downloading E-Mail

Downloading means that you are copying the e-mail from your mail program to your own hard drive or to a floppy disk. To do this, you will first have to:

1. Copy the e-mail from your mail program to your *account directory*. Your account directory is the *directory* where all the files on your account are stored. There will usually be a save or copy command in your menu. Use this command and save the e-mail with a short name (usually up to eight alphanumeric characters).

2. Now exit your mail program and go to the *system prompt* or account directory. Now, if you type **"DIR"** or **"LS"** (for *UNIX*™ systems), you will see a list of all the files on your account. The e-mail that you just saved should be there.

3. Now comes the tricky part. Each system has a different format for downloading files. Contact your local sysop to find out which system you are using. Commonly used systems are *X-Modem*, *Y-Modem*, and *Kermit*. Also find out the necessary commands to download from your account to your hard drive or to a floppy disk.

4. Once you download a file, you can edit it in any word processor or *text editor*. You can then print it out or save the e-mail on disk. Normally,

you will not have to download e-mail, but sometimes you will receive information that you want a *hard copy* of, such as a list of addresses or references.

If you have gotten this far and are able to download e-mail, you have mastered one of the most difficult parts of using the Internet. Again, each system is different, so contact your local sysop or computer center and get detailed instructions on how to download. I have included some of the universal commands, but they may not work for your system.

Deleting, Replying to, and Forwarding E-Mail

You should now know how to read, save, and download e-mail. Other commands you will want to know are how to delete, reply to, and forward e-mail. Deleting e-mail is important if you receive a lot of it. When you receive more e-mail than you have time to read, use the delete command to delete the e-mail that you are not interested in reading. E-mail programs will place some type of marking to indicate that this e-mail has been deleted. After you read your e-mail and/or download it, you will want to delete it so that your account does not fill up. If you use up all the disk space that is allotted to you on your account, future e-mail may be rejected, so it is a good idea to delete the e-mail that you have read or are not interested in. Some Internet accounts will automatically delete your e-mail after a certain amount of time so that you won't have this problem.

When you receive an e-mail, you may want to reply to it. To do this, open up the e-mail and find the reply command. This will allow you to reply to an e-mail without typing in the person's address. In addition, you can include the original contents of the e-mail in your reply. For example, if someone sends a long commentary on a psychological theory, you can select those parts that you agree with or disagree with without retyping the entire letter. It is a good idea to delete the parts of the original e-mail that you are not responding to so that your response is as short as possible. Another feature of the reply command is that the subject line will indicate that you are sending a reply. For example, if someone sent you a survey about your satisfaction with your school's classes, the subject line may say SATISFACTION SURVEY. You can fill out this survey and return it to the original sender without retyping it or knowing his or her address. In the reply, the subject line will say RE: SATISFACTION SURVEY (the RE: stands for "regarding").

The reply command is one of the unique features of e-mail communication. An e-mail can go back and forth between two or more users as many times as you want. It will not only include your latest comments but all the contents of the previous e-mails, so there is no question about who said what.

The last command you will want to know is the forward command. Again, it should be listed in a menu of commands on your screen. The forward command will allow you to forward any e-mail you receive to any other user. For example, if you receive an e-mail regarding a psychology seminar that you feel another user would be interested in or knowledgeable about, you can forward the e-mail to that person. You can even add your own comments such as "I thought you might be interested in this." The other user will see in the subject line that this is an e-mail that you forwarded to him or her. The subject line will say something like FW: SATISFACTION SURVEY (the FW: stands for "forward"). The receiver will see FW: and your address and realize that you forwarded him or her the e-mail. The receiver can then, in turn, reply to or forward the e-mail to whomever he or she wants.

This is the nuts and bolts of e-mail communication. It will most likely be the most productive part of Internet access that you have, so it is a good idea to master these commands as well as the terminology.

You may want to find out how to make copies of the e-mail messages that you send and how to set up an *address book* so that you don't have to remember all the addresses of people that you communicate with. These commands are specific to your system, so you will have to contact your computer center or sysop for instructions.

Internet Activities

1. Learn the commands to save and delete e-mail. Remember, your account may fill up if you don't delete your e-mail regularly.

2. Download and print out an e-mail. Contact your local sysop for the instructions for your system. You will not want to download every e-mail you receive, but knowing how to do so is important when you receive information that you requested and want to include it in your papers or use it as a reference.

3. Have someone send you an e-mail, and use the reply command to send it back. Add a short comment to your response so that he or she knows it is a response from you.

4. Forward an e-mail that you receive to a third party. Add a short comment to it indicating that you are forwarding this e-mail.

   If you have no one to send an e-mail to, feel free to send one to me at DMAHONY@RDZ.STJOHNS.EDU. Let me know what university you are attending and what class you are using this guide for. Also, let me know what you think about the guide. I will send you a response and answer any questions.

CHAPTER 4: E-MAIL DISCUSSION GROUPS

What Are E-Mail Discussion Groups?

E-mail discussion groups, or *lists,* are one of the best sources of information available on the Internet. Discussion groups are an electronic forum where individuals interested in a specific topic get together and communicate with one another. This forum offers two basic services: the ability to distribute a message to a group of people by sending it to a single address, and the option of signing on and off anonymously. You can't participate anonymously, but no one will know when you join a list or when you *signoff* a list.

Discussion groups work through the use of a *listserver,* a program that is set up to "explode" e-mail. For example, if 1,000 people are signed up on a list to discuss Prozac™, you can send an e-mail to the listserver, and it will explode, or copy, your e-mail and send it to all 1,000 of those people. So, let's say that you need information about how Prozac™ is being used to treat Trichotillomania (hair pulling). You search the libraries and find very little information about it because it is a relatively new treatment. What you can do is subscribe to the Prozac™ list and introduce yourself. Let the other subscribers know that you are interested in writing a paper on Prozac™ and Trichotillomania but have not been able to get much information from traditional sources. Also let them know that you would be interested in any information that anyone has on this subject. The responses you get will vary. Researchers on this list may respond and tell you their hypotheses and about ongoing research. They may even point you in the direction of available literature that you have not found. On the other end of the spectrum, you may get Trichotillomania patients who respond to you and tell you what their experiences have been with Prozac™ treatment. This type of personal information is invaluable because no research will fill you in on the details of what the subjective experience is for Trichotillomania patients on Prozac™. They may tell you what side effects they suffer, how effective they feel Prozac™ is, what other types of treatments they have tried, and how useful these treatments have been.

Discussion groups usually revolve around a specific topic. There are discussion groups for cognitive psychology, social psychology, undergraduate students in psychology, depression, anxiety, posttraumatic stress disorder, industrial psychology, statistics, psychodynamic theories, and almost every other area of psychology. A different type of discussion group is the patient discussion group. These groups are considered support groups for people that suffer from a psychiatric disorder or addictive problems. For example, there is a support group for individuals who suffer from schizophrenia. Schizophrenic patients will discuss their symptoms, treatments, experiences in psychiatric hospitals, and in general, what life is like when you suffer from schizophrenia. This is an invaluable resource that you will not find anywhere else. Even if you work in a psychiatric hospital, patients may not tell you the intimacies of their disorders. There are also support groups for alcoholics, drug addicts, sex addicts, and others. These groups exist in addition to traditional support groups. One advantage of these groups is that individuals who live in remote areas of the world can participate, and they can participate whenever they want.

On the other end of the spectrum, there are discussion groups on just about every area of psychology. These groups discuss topics like how to get a research grant, the politics of the field of psychology, and nearly everything else related to psychology.

Discussion Groups Netiquette

Discussion groups, like everything else, have their own etiquette (etiquette on the Internet is commonly referred to as *netiquette*). Once you subscribe to a discussion group, it is a good idea to *lurk* (just read the mail and don't respond) for a while. Get a feeling for what is discussed on the list and who the major participants are. After you have lurked awhile, you can respond to an e-mail that you are interested in, or you can bring up your own topic for discussion. Keep your comments appropriate to the topic of the list. If you are using these discussions for research purposes, you will need to allow yourself some time. Don't subscribe to a list and send out a request the same day requesting some sort of information. If your topic is already under discussion on the list, the other list members will not reply to your request. Even after you lurk for a while and feel comfortable on the list, it may take a couple of days for others to respond to your requests. Some individuals read their e-mail only every couple of days, so they may respond a week or so after you send out a request.

Be polite on these discussion groups. Don't trash what others say. Trashing others on the Internet is known as *flaming* that person. If you flame someone on a discussion group, most likely you will be kicked off. It is all right to disagree with another's views; just be sure you allow them the right to express their views. One reason people subscribe to these lists is so that they can debate issues.

There is also a special language that is used on the Internet. Since you cannot see the person's face that is sending a message, special characters are used to get emotions across to the reader. For example, the :) character is called a *smiley*. If you turn the page sideways, it will look like a smiling face. This is used when someone is expressing happiness on the Internet. The opposite of a smiley is the :(character, which is used to express sadness. If you type in CAPITAL LETTERS on the Internet, it means that you are angry and yelling. Please do not use capitals in discussion groups. They can be easily misinterpreted.

Many abbreviations are used for common expressions. For example, *IMHO* (in my humble opinion) is used on the Internet when you disagree with someone and offer your own opinion. Please use IMHO generously to decrease the likelihood of misunderstandings. *BTW* (by the way) is another common expression on the Internet. You will see other abbreviations as you use the Internet more and more.

Subscribing to a Discussion Group

Two addresses are associated with a discussion group. One is the *listserver address*. This is the address of the computer program that sends out all the e-mail and processes the commands for that particular discussion group. Whenever you want to subscribe to or unsubscribe to a discussion group, you have to send a command to the listserver address. The other address is the *discussion address* that you send your replies or topics of discussion to for everyone to read. Sending messages to the discussion address will copy your message to all the other readers.

We will first go over the commands that you send to the listserver address to subscribe to a discussion group. There are several different list-server programs, and they all use different commands. For most listservers, to subscribe to a discussion group, you have to address the e-mail to the listserver address. You will find the listserver addresses to many discussion groups in Table 4.2. Use the **"subscribe"** command in the body of the e-mail. Do not write anything in the subject line of your e-mail. For example, if you wanted to subscribe to the Prozac™ discussion group, you would send an e-mail with this written in the body of the e-mail:

> **"SUBSCRIBE PROZAC {your name}"**

Replace {your name} in this example with your actual name. Do not include the quotation marks or the braces, do not say please or thank you, and remember to erase any signature that may automatically be included onto your e-mail. In the example, the command is SUBSCRIBE. This will tell the listserver that you want to subscribe to a list. PROZAC is the name of the list that you want to subscribe to. Include a space between each word. Do not write anything else in the body of the e-mail or in the subject line.

At this point, one of two things will happen. Either you will get an e-mail back from mailer-daemon saying that your mail was not delivered or the listserver will send you an e-mail that says you have been subscribed successfully, and it will include a description of what is discussed on the list. If you get the mailer-daemon e-mail, this means that you used the wrong listserver address or the listserver is down. Check the address that you sent it to as well as the syntax of the command you sent. It is always possible that the list no longer exists, so if repeated attempts fail, you should try another list.

To unsubscribe from a discussion group, use the command "signoff {list name}". Table 4.1 lists valid commands for *Listserv* (the most commonly used listserver). If the name on the listserver address is something else, for example, *Listproc* or *Mailbase*, other commands are used. If this is the case, send the "**help**" command in the body of the letter to the listserver address, and you will be sent a list of valid commands for that listserver.

Table 4.1   LISTSERV COMMANDS

Subscribe {list-name yourfirstname yourlastname}	To subscribe to the list, where list-name is the exact name of the list, including hyphens, and then include your name.
Signoff {list-name}	To signoff a list, where list-name is the exact name of the list, including hyphens.
Review {list-name}	To get a list of subscribers, where list-name is the exact name of the list, including hyphens.
Set {list-name} Nomail	This command will stop any mail from being sent to you, where list-name is the exact name of the list, including hyphens. Use this command when you go away for extended periods and do not want your mailbox to fill up.
Set {list-name} Mail	Resume service after an extended leave, where list-name is the exact name of the list, including hyphens.
List	To get a list of all the mailing lists available from this listserver.
Help	To get a list of valid commands along with the correct syntax for this listserver.

When you send any command, remember, do not write anything in the subject line and send it to the listserver address. Many people will send commands to the discussion address, and it will get forwarded to all the persons on the list. Not only will your command not be processed, but you will annoy others on the list.

There are many different listservers with different commands. Usually, when you hear about a list on the Internet, the correct command to subscribe along with the address will be included. Once you subscribe, you will be sent an e-mail with a list of all other valid commands for that particular listserver. Save this e-mail for future reference.

Once you have been subscribed successfully, you will get an e-mail that gives you the discussion address to send your topics of discussion to. This is the second address that I spoke about before. Do not send commands to the discussion address. This address is where you send all of your topics of discussion and replies to.

You will then begin to receive e-mail from this discussion group. The volume of e-mail that you receive will differ on each list. Some lists will send you several e-mails a day, whereas others will send only one a week. It depends on how many people are signed up and how active they are on the list.

Once you are on a discussion group, it is important to *lurk* or *listen in* for a several days. Lurking means that you should just read the e-mail that comes to you until you understand the topics of discussion on a group. If you are unfamiliar with what the group is discussing or it is too complicated for you, try another group. Other readers in the group will not appreciate it if it appears that you do not know what they are discussing.

Once you are on a discussion group, there are two ways that you can respond to someone. Usually, if you are reading an e-mail from the group, you can hit your reply command, type in your reply, and use the send command. You will then be given the option of responding to the whole group or responding to the individual that sent the e-mail. Normally, you should respond to the whole group since they may be interested in your opinion. If someone specifically requests that you reply to him or her alone, then you can reply just to that person. Sometimes people request references regarding a specific subject. For example, if someone requests references about a particular subject and you have references, that person will usually request that you reply directly to him or her since other members on the list may not be interested in these references.

Confidentiality

The power of the Internet resides in its ease of accessibility. Anyone with a computer and a modem can signon. Some of these discussion groups are support groups or patient groups. They usually don't mind if you lurk or even participate, but you should not break the confidentiality of the list. Persons often include their full name and e-mail address in their e-mail. Although they do not expect their messages to be private, they expect that you will not take advantage of this by distributing these e-mails in any inappropriate ways. It is all right to forward them to other interested users or discuss them with colleagues or fellow students, but do not reproduce these discussions in any way that will compromise the person's confidentiality. An example of inappropriate use would be to cite this person's name and address in a paper or journal article.

Viruses

There are many scares on discussion groups about *viruses*. Viruses are computer programs that copy themselves onto other computers and have the ability to destroy files. As of this publication, no viruses are transmittable through e-mail. Eventually, you may get letters saying that various viruses are transmitted through e-mail. This is a hoax. Please do not forward these letters to other users.

Table 4.2 lists discussion group addresses.

Internet Activities

1. Signon to one or two discussion groups that you are interested in. Keep in mind that some lists are more active than others, so you may get one message a week or 30 messages each day. If you get many messages, make sure that you delete them daily so that they do not fill up your mailbox. If your mailbox is full, new messages will get rejected.

2. Read and save the introductory e-mail that is sent to you. It will tell you what discussions are appropriate on the list and all the relevant commands that you can send to the listserver.

3. After you have lurked for a while on a discussion group, reply to one of the messages that you are interested in, or send out your own message about a new topic.

4. Read and answer any responses you get from your message.

Table 4.2   DISCUSSION GROUP ADDRESSES

LIST NAME	COMMAND ADDRESS	TOPIC
AABT_COMPUTER_ SIG-L (one word)	LISTSERV@UNM.EDU	Computers special interest group of AABT
ADDICT-L	LISTSERV@KENTVM.BITNET	Discussion of addiction
AERA-GSL	LISTSERV@ASUVM.INRE.ASU.EDU	Devoted to issues of graduate education and support
ALCOHOL	LISTSERV@LMUACAD.BITNET	Alcohol and drug studies
ALZHEIMER	MAJORDOMO@WUBIOS.WUSTL.EDU Use e-mail address instead of name for majordomo	Alzheimer's discussion
APASD-L	LISTSERV@VTVM1.BITNET	APA Research Psychology
APASSC	LISTSERV@GWUVM.BITNET	APA Science Student Council
APHAMH-L	LISTSERV@BROWNVM.BROWN.EDU	Mental health from a public health perspective
APSSCNET	LISTSERV@MCGILL1.BITNET	American Psychological Society Student Caucus
ARLIST-L	ARLIST@PSY.UQ.OZ.AU LISTPROC@SCU.EDU.AU	Organizational psychology applied action research

LIST NAME	COMMAND ADDRESS	TOPIC
AUTISM	LISTSERV@SJUVM.BITNET	SJU autism and developmental disabilities
BEHAV-AN	LISTSERV@VM1.NODAK.EDU	Behavior analysis discussion group
BEHAVIOR	LISTSERV@ASUACAD.BITNET	Behavioral and emotional disorders in children
BEHAVIOR ANALYSIS (one word)	BEHAVIORANALYSIS-REQUEST@MANKATO.MSUS.EDU	Behavior analysis discussion group
BISEXU-L	LISTSERV@BROWNVM.BITNET	Bisexuality discussion
BMDP-L	LISTSERV@MCGILL1.BITNET or LISTSERV@VM1.MCGILL.CA	BMDP discussion list
BRAIN-L	LISTSERV@MCGILL1.BITNET or LISTSERV@VM1.MCGILL.CA	Mind-brain discussion group
BRAINTMR	BRAINTMR-REQUEST@MITVMA.MIT.EDU	Brain tumor discussion list
BRUNSWIK	LISTSERV@ALBNYVM1.BITNET	Brunswikian psychology and social judgment
CAVEAT-L	LISTPROC@FHS.CSU.MCMASTER.CA	Violence prevention and treatment

LIST NAME	COMMAND ADDRESS	TOPIC
CHILD ABUSE	LISTSERV@UBVM.BITNET	Forum for professionals for discussion of topics related to child abuse
CMDNET	LISTSERV@KSUVM.BITNET	Conflict management division list
COGDEVEL	LISTSERV@UNCCVM.BITNET	Cognitive development discussion
COMPSY-L	LISTSERV@UIUCVMD.BITNET	Midwest forum for community/ecological psychology
COUNPSY	LISTSERV@UGA.CC.UGA.EDU	Counseling psychologists list
Cussnet	CUSSNET-REQUEST@STAT.COM	Computer users in social sciences
DIV12	LISTSERV@VM1.NODAK.EDU	APA'S Division 12 (Clinical Division)
DIV28	LISTSERV@GWUVM.BITNET	APA's Division 28
DOWN-SYN	LISTSERV@VM1.NODAK.EDU	Down's Syndrome discussion
EARLI-AE	LISTSERV@HEARN.BITNET	European association for research on learning and instruction
ECUPSY-L	LISTSERV@ECUVM1.BITNET	Psychology department faculty, staff, and students

LIST NAME	COMMAND ADDRESS	TOPIC
E-MAIL LISTS	Send a message to: IceT@Mail.utexas.edu to receive this list	This is a list of e-mail discussion groups compiled by Tor Neilands, this is not a listserver
ENVBEH-L	ENVBEH-L@POLYVM.BITNET or LISTPROC@DUKE.POLY.EDU	Forum on environment and human behavior
ETHOLOGY	LISTSERV@SEARN.SURENET.SE	Discussion of animal behavior and behavioral ecology
FACES-L	LISTSERV@UTEPA.BITNET	Interdisciplinary study of faces
FAMCOMM	COMSERVE@RPITSVM.BITNET	Marital/family and relational communication
FAMLYSCI	LISTSERV@UKCC.UKY.EDU	Family science, marriage, family therapy, family sociology, and behavioral aspect of family medicine
Feminist International Psychology List	Irene Hanson Frieze, PhD frieze@vms.cis.pitt.edu Send your e-mail address if you would like to be added to the list, it is not an automated list, so standard listserver commands won't work	Psychology of Women Division of the American Psychological Association
FORENS-L	MAILSERV@FAUVAX.BITNET	Forensic medicine and sciences interest group

LIST NAME	COMMAND ADDRESS	TOPIC
FORPSY-L	LISTSERV@MIZZOU1.BITNET	Discussion of issues in forensic psychiatry
GANGSTM	GANGTM-REQUEST@DHVX20.CSUDH.EDU	Discussion of gangs and gang-related problems
GENDER	MAJORDOMO@INDIANA.EDU	Discussing gender issues
GERINET	LISTSERV@UBVM.BITNET	Geriatric health care discussion group
GSS-L	LISTSERV@UGA.BITNET	Group support systems
IAPSY-L	LISTSERV@ALBNYVM1.BITNET	Interamerican psychologists list (SIPNET)
ICTAB-L	LISTSERV@UNM.EDU	Clinical researchers and clinicians interested in the area of addictive behaviors
INTVIO-L	LISTSERV@URIACC.URI.EDU	Intimate violence research and practice
IOOB-L	LISTSERV@UGA.BITNET	Industrial psychology
IOOBF-L	LISTSERV@UGA.BITNET	Industrial psychology

LIST NAME	COMMAND ADDRESS	TOPIC
Latin-psych	LISTSERV@NETCOM.COM	Una lista de psiquiatras y psicologos en el Internet en lo que la diferencia de otras es que el idioma principal es el Espanol, y se estimula la discusion de las experiencias unicas de los distintos paises de latinoamerica e ibericos desde el punto de vista de la salud mental
LGBPSYCH	NEIL@PSYCH.MCGILL.CA	Discussion among lesbian, gay, and bisexual graduate students in psychology
MACPSYCH	MACPSYCH-REQUEST@STOLAF.EDU	Psychologists and others interested in using the Macintosh in research and teaching
MADNESS	MADNESS@SJUVM.STJOHNS.EDU	Forum for people who suffer from schizophrenia, bipolar disorder, etc.
MOTORDEV	LISTSERV@UMDD.BITNET	Human motor skill development
MPSYCH-L	LISTSERV@BROWNVM.BITNET	Society for Mathematical Psychology
NEURO1-L	LISTSERV@UICVM.BITNET	Neuroscience information
NEURON	NEURON-REQUEST@CATTELL.PSYCH.UPENN.EDU	All aspects of neural networks (and any type of network or neuromorphic system)
NEUROPSYCH	MAILBASE@MAILBASE.AC.UK	Neuropsychology discussion

LIST NAME	COMMAND ADDRESS	TOPIC
NEUROPSYCH-HIV-AIDS	ELIOT@NETCOM.COM	Neuropsychological disorders in persons with AIDS; professionals only
OBLOMOV	LISTPROC@RUG.NL	Psychological research on academic and general procrastination
ORGMGT-1	Contact list owner at: HEES@SISWO.UVA.NL	List concerning organizational and management studies
ORGCULT	Contact list owner at ORGCULT@COMMERCE.UQ.EDU.AU	Discussion group about organizational culture and organizational change issues
OUR-KIDS (Developmental Delays)	MAJORDOMA@TBAG.OSC.EDU	Developmental delays discussion
OUTCMTEN	LISTSERV@SJUVM.STJOHNS.EDU	Discussion about problems of assessing and analyzing outcomes of interventions aimed at improving mental health
PARKINSN	LISTSERV@VM.UTCC.UTORONTO.CA	Parkinson's disease discussion group
PCP	MAILBASE@MAILBASE.AC.UK	Forum for the discussion of personal construct psychology

LIST NAME	COMMAND ADDRESS	TOPIC
PENDULUM (Bipolar disorder)	MAJORDOMO@NCAR.UCAR.EDU use address	Bipolar discussion group
PNI	LISTSERV@CCAT.SAS.UPENN.EDU	This list's focus is on past, present, and future research in psychoneuroimmunology and neural-immune relations
PRACTICE	MAJORDOMO@LISTS.APA.ORG	Practice directory list to discuss issues facing practicing psychologists; APA members only
PREVIEW	COMSERVE@RPITSVM.BITNET	Current research in human communication
Prozac	LISTSERV@SJUVM.STJOHNS.EDU	Discussion for persons taking or interested in Prozac
PSI-L	LISTSERV@RPITSVM.BITNET	Parapsychology discussion
PSTAT-L	LISTSERV@IRLEARN.BITNET	Discussion of stats and programming
PSYART	LISTSERV@NERVM.BITNET	Institute for Psychological Study of the Art
PSYCGRAD	LISTSERV@UOTTAWA.BITNET LISTSERV@ACADVM1.UOTTAWA.CA	Psychology graduate students discussion group
PSYCH	LISTSERV@PSUVM.BITNET	Psychology department

LIST NAME	COMMAND ADDRESS	TOPIC
PSYCH-COUNS	MAILBASE@MAILBASE.AC.UK	Discussion group for people interested in theoretical or research issues in counseling and psychotherapy
PSYCH-L	LISTSERV@UOTTAWA.BITNET	UOTTAWA School of Psychology discussion list
PSYCHE-D	LISTSERV@IRIS.RFMH.ORG	Interdisciplinary study of consciousness and the brain
PSYCHTALK	LISTSERV@FRE.FSU.UMD.EDU	A forum for undergraduates in psychology; open to all topics in psychology
PSYCINFO LIST	PSYCINFO@LISTS.APA.ORG Send an e-mail to this site; this is not a listserver	Tips and techniques used to search psychological research literature
PSYLAW-L	LISTSERV@UTEPA.BITNET	Psychology and law; international discussion
PSYMEA-L	LISTSERV@UBVM.BITNET	Developmental psychology
PsyNetCa	PSYNETCA@AOL.COM send subject line: *Request Info*	California Psychologist Internet Mail Group; moderator (PsyNet is not associated with the APA PsychNET, but is rather a loose coalition of licensed, practicing psychologists networking via e-mail)

LIST NAME	COMMAND ADDRESS	TOPIC
PsyNetUSA	PSYNETUSA@AOL.COM	PsyNetUSA has been formed to network psychologists in the challenging environment of today's practice
	Request for PsyNetUSA information with the message in the body of your e-mail: [yourfirstname yourlastname yourdegree] [your professional affiliation] [your state or province]	
PSYSTS-L	PSYSTS-L@MIZZOU1.BITNET	Psychology statistics discussion
QUALRS-L	LISTSERV@UGA.BITNET	Qualitative research for the human sciences
RECOVERY	RECOVERY@WVNVM.WVNET.EDU	Survivors of childhood sexual abuse
SAS-L	LISTSERV@UGA.CC.UGA.EDU	SAS-specific programming, statistics questions, and discussion list
SCHIZ-L	LISTSERV@UMAB.UMD.EDU	Devoted to providing a forum for communications among schizophrenia researchers
SCHIZOPH	LISTSERV@UTORONTO.BITNET or LISTSERV@UBVM.CC.BUFFALO.EDU	Forum for anyone who wishes to discuss issues related to schizophrenia
SCR-L	SCR-L@MIZZOU1.BITNET	Study of cognitive rehabilitation
SEXADD-L	SEXADD-L-REQUEST@KENTVM.KENT.EDU	Forum that discusses all aspects of sexual addiction

LIST NAME	COMMAND ADDRESS	TOPIC
SEXTALK	LISTSERV@TAMVM1.TAMU.EDU	Issues related to sexuality
SLFHLP-L	LISTSERV@UIUCVMD.BITNET	Self-help research discussion group
SLFHLP-L	LISTSERV@VMD.CSO.UIUC.EDU	International discussion group for researchers in self-help/mutual aid
SMOKE-FREE	LISTSERV@RA.MSSTATE.EDU	Tobacco addiction discussion group
SPORTPSY	LISTSERV@TEMPLEVM.BITNET	Exercise and sports psychology
SPSSI-L	SPSSI-L@VMS.CIS.PITT.EDU	Society for the Psychological Study of Social Issues
SPSSX-L	LISTSERV@UGA.CC.UGA.EDU	SPSS-specific programming and statistics questions
STAT-L	LISTSERV@MCGILL1.BITNET	Statistical consulting
Stat-l	LISTSERV@UGA.CC.UGA.EDU	General statistical questions and problems
STOPRAPE	LISTSERV@BROWNVM.BITNET	Sexual assault activist list
STUTT-L	LISTSERV@TEMPLEVM.BITNET	Stuttering: research and clinical practice
SUBSTANCE-RELATED-DISORDERS	LISTSERV@NETCOM.COM	Substance-related disorders

LIST NAME	COMMAND ADDRESS	TOPIC
Suicide List	JO@SAMARITANS.ORG For anonymous posts, send e-mail to: SAMARITANS@ANON.PENET.FI This list is not a listserver, so do not use any commands; state in the body of the e-mail that you would like to subscribe	Suicidal feelings and thoughts
SUICIDE-SUPPORT	LISTSERV@RESEARCH.CANON.OZ.AU	Suicide support discussion group
SUPPORT	LISTSERV@SJUVM.STJOHNS.EDU	General support group
TBI-SPRT	LISTSERV@SJUVM.STJOHNS.EDU	Brain injuries support group
TCAN	LISTSERV@ETSUADMN.ETSU.EDU	Discussion list for Texas counselors, counselor educators, and counselor supervisors
TIPS	LISTSERV@FRE.FSU.UMD.EDU	All aspects of teaching in psychology are covered
TRANSGEN	LISTSERV@BROWNVM.BROWN.EDU	Transgender discussion group
TRAUMATIC STRESS	TRAUMATIC-STRESS@NETCOM.COM	Promotes the investigation, assessment, and treatment of the immediate and long-term psychosocial, biophysiological, and existential consequences of highly stressful (traumatic) events

LIST NAME	COMMAND ADDRESS	TOPIC
TTM	MAJORDOMO@CS.COLUMBIA.EDU	Trichotillomania discussion group
UG-PSYCHLIST	UG-PSYCHLIST-REQUEST@PSY.UQ.OZ.AU With the word "**subscribe**" as the only content of your message; no name or address needed	List for undergraduate psychology students (majors and minors)
VALIDATA	LISTSERV@UA1VM.BITNET	Measurement and scales
VIRTPSY	LISTSERV@SJUVM.STJOHNS.EDU	Students of psychology interested in the social contracts and interactions within the environments known as virtual reality
WALKERS-IN-DARKNESS (Depression)	WALKERS-REQUEST@WORLD.STD.COM	Depression discussion

CHAPTER 5: ON-LINE JOURNALS

What Are On-Line Journals?

On-line journals are also available through listservers. Unlike discussion groups, on-line journals are usually not interactive; that is, they will send you the journals periodically, but you can't reply directly. On-line journals are a growing resource on the Internet. The advantage of them over traditional journals is that you will receive state-of-the-art research, not something that was conducted two or three years ago. Further, the author's e-mail address will usually be included, so if you want to comment on the study or request additional information, you can send him or her an e-mail. Some on-line journals are peer reviewed and have a status equal to traditional journals. Be aware of the peer-review status before you cite a study.

On-line journals, as well as the discussion groups, will all have an address you can send to for previous issues or discussions. This information will be included in the introductory e-mail that is sent to you when you successfully subscribe.

Table 5.1 lists on-line journal addresses.

Internet Activity

1. Signon to one or two of the on-line journals. Keep in mind that these journals are not like discussion groups where you can reply to them. Read the journals, and decide whether or not the information that they discuss is important to you. Unsubscribe from the journals that you are not interested in.

Table 5.1   ON-LINE JOURNAL ADDRESSES

PSYC	LISTSERV@PUCC.BITNET	PSYCOLOQUY: refereed electronic journal of psychology
PSYCHE-L	LISTSERV@IRIS.RFMH.ORG	PSYCHE: a journal of research on consciousness
PSYGRD-J	LISTSERV@UOTTAWA.BITNET or LISTSERV@ACADVM1.UOTTAWA.CA	The Psychology Graduate-Student Journal
The TRAUMATOLOGY e-journal	Please write to: trauma@netcom.com and request to be added to this list since listserver commands will not work	Journal on trauma

CHAPTER 6: USENET NEWSGROUPS?

What Are Usenet Newsgroups?

Usenet newsgroups are usually considered to be the heart of the Internet. These discussion groups are similar to the e-mail discussion groups except that the format is different. Usenet newsgroups are electronic bulletin boards where all the messages are posted instead of sending them out to subscribers. Calling them newsgroups is a misnomer since they don't often contain news. More than 5,000 newsgroups discuss everything from music to biology. Much like the e-mail discussion groups, interested persons can read, respond to, or post messages on these groups. The difference is that the newsgroups are more like an electronic bulletin board. When you access a newsgroup, you will see a list of messages and a short title for each message. You can browse down the list and choose only the messages that you want to read.

Accessing Newsgroups

To access the newsgroups, you have to:

1. Use the menu system from your Internet access account to access Usenet newsgroups. If you do not have a menu system, type "**NN**" or "**RN**" at the prompt. Be patient. Because of the way that newsgroups work, it will take a minute or so to load them up. If none of those commands work, contact your sysop or local computer center for the command to access the newsgroups. Some Internet access accounts will not have access to all the newsgroups.

2. Once you are in the newsgroups, a menu should appear at the bottom or top of your screen. There will be search commands and browse commands. If they are not there, you will have to find out the commands from your sysop or computer center. Use these commands to search for a specific newsgroup or page up and down the list. The search command is useful if you know the newsgroup that you want to access because there are more than 5,000 newsgroups to look through.

3. To access a newsgroup, place the cursor on it and hit the Enter key. You will then have to wait while the computer loads the messages from that newsgroup. You will then see a list of all the messages or postings to that newsgroup. To read a posting, place the cursor on it and hit Enter.

The same netiquette applies for the newsgroups as for the e-mail discussion groups. Read the *FAQ* (frequently asked questions) document posting to find out what is and what is not an appropriate topic for a particular newsgroup. The FAQ posting will usually be one of the first messages on the newsgroup and will answer many of your questions so that you don't have to ask other newsgroup readers. If it is not one of the first messages, scroll down the list and look for it.

Helpful Commands

You will then need to learn several commands, all of which should be at the bottom or top of your screen. Since there are dozens of Usenet programs, not everyone will use the same commands. There are too many different commands to list them all here; just remember that the commands you will need should be listed at the bottom or top of your screen. If they are not, ask your sysop. You will need to know the commands to read, reply, download, and post. To read a posting, just place the cursor on it and hit Enter. Once you are reading a posting, you may want to respond to it. Look for the reply command on your screen. You will then be given a copy of the original posting in which you can type your reply. You can edit the original posting so that only the relevant material is included in your response. Once you finish, find the send command to post your response onto the newsgroup. People all over the world will now see that there is a response to the original message, and they will be able to read it and respond to it. This is typically how people communicate on newsgroups. Often you will see a posting with 10 or 15 responses. Called a *thread*, this is a long discussion about a particular topic.

Downloading and Posting

Other commands you'll want to know are downloading and posting.

Downloading is done by saving the posting. You can save one or several at one time. You need to use whatever save command your system uses. When you save a posting, you will be asked to give it a name. Give it a short name that you can easily remember. For example, to save an article about social psychology, save it as "social". Once you save it, the posting will be in your local directory on your Internet account. You will then have to follow instructions on your local account to download it to a disk or print it out.

Posting messages should be done only after you have read the FAQ and understand what is appropriate to post on a particular newsgroup. Find the post command to post a letter, and follow the instructions. You can type in a posting or *upload* something that you have already written. (Uploading means to send something that you've already written to the newsgroup.) Your message will then be posted for all other users to see and respond to.

Table 6.1 lists psychology newsgroup addresses.

Internet Activities

1. Find out the command to access the newsgroups on your account. Access the newsgroups and browse around.

2. Read the FAQs for the newsgroups that you are interested in to determine what is discussed on that newsgroup.

3. Download a posting from a newsgroup and print it out. Many lengthy postings on the newsgroups outline psychological theories or research projects that you can use as a reference in your papers.

Table 6.1   PSYCHOLOGY NEWSGROUP ADDRESSES

TOPIC	NEWSGROUP
Perception, memory, judgment, and reasoning	sci.cognitive
Dialog and news in psychiatry and psychobiology	sci.med.psychobiology
General psychology	sci.psychology
Research issues in psychology	sci.psychology.research
Digest of general issues in psychology	sci.psychology.digest
Psyche Electronic Journal	sci.psychology.journals.psyche
Adlerian Psychology	alt.psychology.adlerian
General help with psychological problems	alt.psychology.help
Personality taxonomies/assessment/models	alt.psychology.personality
NLP	alt.psychology.nlp
Mistake Theory	alt.psychology.mistake-theory
Recovering from all types of abuse	alt.abuse.recovery
Recovery for abuse offenders/perpetrators	alt.abuse.offender.recovery
Alternate models of dealing with abuse	alt.abuse.transcendence
General topics in recovery	alt.recovery
Recovery and Alcoholics Anonymous	alt.recovery.aa

TOPIC	NEWSGROUP
Recovery and Narcotics Anonymous	alt.recovery.na
Recovering from sexual addictions	alt.recovery.addiction.sexual
Codependency	alt.recovery.codependency
Recovering from the effects of religion	alt.recovery.religion
Recovery from Catholicism in specific	alt.recovery.catholicism
Recovering from sexual abuse	alt.sexual.abuse.recovery
	alt.sexual.abuse.recovery.d
Moderated version:alt.sexual.abuse.recovery	alt.abuse-recovery
Partners of sexual abuse survivors	alt.support.abuse-partners
Anxiety and panic disorders	alt.support.anxiety-panic
Arthritis	alt.support.arthritis
Asthma	alt.support.asthma
Attention-deficit disorders	alt.support.attn-deficit
Fat-acceptance with no dieting talk	alt.support.big-folks
Self-acceptance for fat people/no diet talk	soc.support.fat-acceptance
Cancer	alt.support.cancer
Cerebral palsy	alt.support.cerebral-palsy
Crohn's/ulcerative colitis/irritable bowel	alt.support.crohns-colitis
Depression and mood disorders	alt.support.depression
Manic depression and bipolar disorders	alt.support.depression.manic
Development delay	alt.support.dev-delays
Parents and family of children with diabetes	alt.support.diabetes.kids
Dieting/losing weight/nutrition	alt.support.diet
Persons w/ dissociative disorders (e.g., -MPD)	alt.support.dissociation
Divorce/marital breakups	alt.support.divorce
Dystonia (abnormal muscle spasms)	alt.support.dystonia
Eating disorders (anorexia, bulimia, etc.)	alt.support.eating-disord
Epilepsy	alt.support.epilepsy
Former cult members and family and friends	alt.support.ex-cult
Issues of grief and loss	alt.support.grief
Disorders of migraine and headache ailments	alt.support.headaches.migraine
Learning disabilities (e.g., -dyslexia)	alt.support.learning-disab
Loneliness	alt.support.loneliness
Multiple sclerosis	alt.support.mult-sclerosis
Effects of second-hand smoke	alt.support.non-smokers
Obesity	alt.support.obesity
Obsessive-compulsive disorder (OCD)	alt.support.ocd
For people with ostomies (surgical proc.)	alt.support.ostomy
For people with personality disorders	alt.support.personality
Post-polio syndrome	alt.support.post-polio
Individuals with prostatitis	alt.support.prostate.prostatitis
Issues of interest to short people, including dwarfism	alt.support.short
Shyness	alt.support.shyness

TOPIC	NEWSGROUP
Sleep disorders and problems sleeping	alt.support.sleep-disorder
Spina-bifida	alt.support.spina-bifida
Help being a step-parent	alt.support.step-parents
Stopping or quitting smoking	alt.support.stop-smoking
Stuttering and other speaking difficulties	alt.support.stuttering
Issues of interest to tall people, including Marfan syndrome	alt.support.tall
Tinnitus/ringing ears/other head noises	alt.support.tinnitus
Tourette's syndrome	alt.support.tourette
Transgendered and intersexed persons	soc.support.transgendered alt.transgendered
Gay youths helping each other	soc.support.youth.gay-lesbian-bi
All other support topics and questions	alt.support
Angst	alt.angst
Self-improvement tips and techniques	alt.self-improve
General discussion of suicide and techniques	alt.suicide.holiday
Suicide/depression around final exams	alt.suicide.finals
Autism	bit.listserv.autism
Downs syndrome	bit.listserv.down-syn
Computer access for persons with disabilities	bit.listserv.easi
Psychology graduate students	bit.listserv.psycgrad
Exercise and sports psychology	bit.listserv.sportpsy
Traumatic brain injury (TBI)	bit.listserv.tbi-support

CHAPTER 7: ACCESSING INFORMATION USING GOPHER

What Is Gopher?

Gopher is a *menu-driven system*, developed by the University of Minnesota, that allows you to go all over the world in search of information. A menu-driven system is a system of interconnected menus that allows you to "burrow" deeper and deeper until you find the information that you are looking for.

Gopher was designed to find and download computer files that are on FTP sites without having to learn all the complicated FTP commands. FTP sites are computers that are accessible by the public, via the Internet, and contain information that you can download. They include things like journal articles and books as well as pictures and software programs. (For a full description of FTP, see Chapter 9.)

Using Gopher, you can download text, graphics, and *program files*. Text files are files that have text (words) in them. Graphics files are files that have graphics or pictures in them. You will need to obtain the appropriate software to view these graphics files. Program files are files that contain software. Psychological testing scoring programs, games, and just about any other type of program that you can imagine are available.

So, let's say you want to find information on psychological research, and a Gopher site exists that puts all the available information on a menu. Now, let's say that someone else is interested in information on clinical psychology, and a Gopher site exists that puts all that information on a menu. If these two menu systems are connected, anyone that accesses one menu can access the other. Now imagine that thousands of specialized Gopher sites are interconnected. This is exactly what Gopher is, and all these interconnected menus are called *Gopherspace*.

What this means is that if you have access to one Gopher site, you can access any other Gopher site. Gopher is much more user friendly than FTP because you can use the menus to find what you are interested in. In addition, Gopher will find the file and put it on your screen for you to read.

Gopher is very simple; its purpose was to make the Internet easier to access.

Accessing Gopher Sites

1. To access Gopher, follow instructions on your menu system, or type "**gopher**" at the prompt. You will then go into your *root menu*, the menu

system that you connect to when you access Gopher. It will usually be a menu about your university if you are accessing from a university. Your root menu will give you a list of different Gopher sites that you can access, or you can go to any Gopher site that you know the address of.

2. If you would like to access a site other than your root menu, when you go into Gopher, type "**gopher {address}**", where address is the address of a valid Gopher site. With some systems, you do not have to type in the word *gopher*. Consult your sysop if you have difficulty with this command. Using this command, you will go directly to any Gopher site (assuming it still exists) you have the correct address of.

When you go into your root menu, or any other menu, you will see a list of entries. At the end of each entry on the menu there will be a symbol that indicates where that entry will lead you. If / (a slash) follows the entry, it means that this entry leads to another menu. If . (a period) follows the entry, it means that the entry leads to a text, graphic, or program file.

Keep in mind that much like the rest of the Internet, you will run into dead ends in Gopher. Many times you will get an error message. This can mean many things, including a power outage, a busy phone line, and a computer that is down. If you get an error message, try the site at a later time. Sites can also disappear forever, so don't be frustrated if you can't find a site that you once could; look elsewhere for the information.

Menus at Gopher Sites

Once you go to a Gopher site of interest, you will be given a menu of that site. You can go up and down the menu by using the up and down arrow keys on your keyboard. If you find something of interest on the menu, place the cursor over it and press the Enter key or the right arrow key. You will go either to another menu or to a file. (To go back to the previous menu, press "**U**".) When you go into a text file, you will see it right on your screen. You will then be given several options. Press "**R**" to return, or exit, the file you're looking at; "**M**" to mail the file to yourself or someone else; "**S**" to save the file in your account directory; and "**P**" to print the file (this will not print out on your printer at home, but rather on your computer center's printer). Remember, these commands may not work on your system. If they don't, contact your sysop or your local computer center (see Table 7.1).

That's about it for Gopher. Because it was designed for ease of use, there aren't any complicated commands. Follow the menu system, and use the commands on your screen to navigate around Gopher. You will even run into Gopher sites that will do searches for you. When you get to one of these sites, type in the subject that you are interested in, and it will search Gopher sites for the subject you requested.

Using Gopher, you can also "go to" libraries all over the world and access their card catalogue systems to see if they have a book that you want.

Table 7.2 lists Gopher site addresses.

Table 7.1   GOPHER COMMANDS

gopher (address)	Go to a Gopher site where address is the exact Gopher site address. With some systems, you do not need to type in the word *gopher*. Contact your sysop if you have difficulty with this command.
Up arrow	Go up a Gopher menu.
Down arrow	Go down a Gopher menu.
U	Go to previous menu.
M	When viewing a text file, this command will mail the file to any e-mail account.
S	When viewing any file, this command will save it to your account directory.
P	When viewing a text file, this command will print the file to a printer. Usually, it will be printed out at the university computer center.
Left arrow	Exits an item and returns you to the previous menu.

Internet Activities

1. Enter Gopherspace and look around.

2. Find a text file that interests you and download it.

3. Find a Gopher menu that will conduct a search for you, and use it to search for something that interests you.

Table 7.2   GOPHER SITE ADDRESSES

NLM—CPS Screening for Abnormal Bereavement
gopher://gopher.nlm.nih.gov:70/00/hstat/guide_cps/TEMPgrp10/cps50.txt

National Institute of Mental Health—You are Not Alone/Mental Illness
gopher://gopher.gsa.gov:70/00/staff/pa/cic/health/youalone

National Institute of Mental Health—Consumer Information
gopher://gopher.gsa.gov:70/00/staff/pa/cic/health/

National Institute of Mental Health—Obsessive-Compulsive Disorder
gopher://gopher.gsa.gov:70/00/staff/pa/cic/health/obsess

National Institute of Mental Health—Schizophrenia: Questions and Answers
gopher://gopher.gsa.gov:70/00/staff/pa/cic/health/schizo

The Self Help Center
gopher://MIZZOU1.MISSOURI.EDU:801/1213760

Self Help info University of Illinois
gopher://gopher.uiuc.edu:70/11/UI/CSF/Coun/SHB

NLM—CPS Screening for Suicidal Intent
gopher://gopher.nlm.nih.gov:70/00/hstat/guide_cps/TEMPgrp10/cps53.txt

The gopher at Catholic University of America maintains a "Test Locator" that is a searchable resource of information on a wide variety of published tests.

    Host: vmsgopher.cua.edu
    Path: /special resources/ERIC Clearinghouse on Evaluation and
            Assessment/Test Locator

    The Test Locator contains several useful resources. The Educational Testing Service Test Collection database contains records on more than 9,500 tests and research instruments. The records describe the tests and tell where they are available. The Buros Test Review Locator tells which of the Buros Mental Measurements Yearbooks contains reviews of a specific test. The PRO-ED Test Review database contains records that indicate which volume of "Test Critiques" contains the review of a test that you identified.

National Institute of Mental Health Gopher
gopher://gopher.nimh.nih.gov/1

The American Psychological Society software archive is at
gopher.hanover.edu.

Washington and Lee University—What's new in psychology
gopher://liberty.uc.wlu.edu:70/11/internet/new_internet
gopher://liberty.uc.wlu.edu:70/11/internet

Harvard Clinical Psychology Gopher
gopher://count51.med.harvard.edu:70/11/.clinical/.psych

University of Miami Psychology Gopher
gopher://caldmed.med.miami.edu:70/11/.gopher/discipline/
Discipline-Specific%20Sources/Psychiatry%20and%20Psychology

Washington and Lee University Mental Health Gopher
gopher://honor.uc.wlu.edu:1020/1%20%20%23bf/cl

Psychiatric Resource page at Yale
gopher://info.med.yale.edu:70/11/Disciplines/Discipline/Psychiatry

National Institute of Mental Health—Dealing with the Angry Child
gopher://gopher.gsa.gov:70/00/staff/pa/cic/children/angry

Psychology Electronic Journals
gopher://ucsbuxa.ucsb.edu:3001/11/.Journals

EATING DISORDERS National Institute of Mental Health—Eating Disorders
gopher://gopher.gsa.gov:70/00/staff/pa/cic/health/disorder

DRUG RELATED CPS Screening for Alcohol and Other Drug Abuse
gopher://gopher.nlm.nih.gov:70/00/hstat/guide_cps/TEMPgrp10/cps55.txt

NCADI—National Clearinghouse for Alcohol and Drug Information
gopher://cyfer.esusda.gov:70/11/CYFER-net/resources/substance

National Institute of Mental Health—On Depression
gopher://gopher.gsa.gov:70/00/staff/pa/cic/health/letstalk.txt
gopher://gopher.gsa.gov:70/00/staff/pa/cic/health/depress

DEMENTIA NLM—CPS Screening for Dementia
gopher://gopher.nlm.nih.gov:70/00/hstat/guide_cps/TEMPgrp10/cps50.txt

DEPRESSION: NLM—CPS Screening for Depression
gopher://gopher.nlm.nih.gov:70/00/hstat/guide_cps/TEMPgrp10/cps52.txt

National Library of Medicine on depression
gopher://gopher.nlm.nih.gov:70/11/hstat/ahcpr/depress

National Library of Medicine—clinical practice guidelines
gopher://gopher.nlm.nih.gov:70/11/hstat/ahcpr/depress/TEMPgrp1

National Institute of Mental Health—Panic Disorder
gopher://gopher.gsa.gov:70/00/staff/pa/cic/health/panic

AIDS
Psychological Effects of Aids—1,275 citations
gopher://gopher.nlm.nih.gov:70/00/bibs/cbm/psycaids.txt

PAVNET—Partners Against Violence
gopher://cyfer.esusda.gov:70/11/violence

National Data Archive on Child Abuse and Neglect
gopher://gopher.fldc.cornell.edu:70/

National Institute of Mental Health—Plain Talk about Wife Abuse
gopher://gopher.gsa.gov:70/00/staff/pa/cic/health/wabuse

BOSTON UNIVERSITY
Counseling Center
gopher://gopher.bu.edu:70/00/Who%2c%20What%2c%20Where%2c%20When/
University%20Departments/Counseling%20Services/Counseling%20Center

PURDUE UNIVERSITY
Psychological Services Center (and Student Health)
gopher oasis.cc.purdue.edu 2525
Select "Mental Health" from the main menu

STATE UNIVERSITY OF NEW YORK AT BUFFALO Counseling Center
gopher wings.buffalo.edu
From the main menu, select "Student Life and Services"
Then select "Counseling Center"

UNIVERSITY OF ILLINOIS, URBANA-CHAMPAIGN Counseling Center
gopher gopher.uiuc.edu
From the main menu, select "Univ. of Illinois at U-C Campus Information"
Then select "Campus Services"
And finally select "Counseling Service"

CHAPTER 8: THE WORLD WIDE WEB

What Is the World Wide Web?

The World Wide Web, commonly referred to as the WWW or the Web, is the most sophisticated Internet access available. It incorporates every other Internet program, such as Gopher, Usenet, and FTP, in a user-friendly environment that includes pictures and sounds. The WWW works by linking documents with something called *hypertext*. Using hypertext, you can read one document and go directly to other related documents. For example, if you are reading an on-line journal that has a reference to another journal article, you can go straight to the other article without knowing where it is. You can therefore bounce around from document to document without using difficult commands and without knowing the addresses of all the documents.

Much like the other programs mentioned here, access to the WWW depends on how your Internet access provider is connected and what programs it uses. The WWW is accessed through a program called a *browser*. A browser can read documents, download documents, read Usenet newsgroups, access Gopher sites, and more.

The most sophisticated access methods to the WWW usually use one of two graphical browsers, Mosaic™ or Netscape™. These browsers allow you to access the WWW in full color; they allow you to view pictures and to hear sounds. To use a graphical browser, you usually need a special account called a *SLIP* or *PPP connection*. Setting up graphical browsers in SLIP or PPP accounts is too complicated (and there are too many types) to explain in this guide, but interested users should speak to their sysop for detailed instructions. Most systems use a *text browser*. Text browsers access everything on the WWW that graphical browsers do, but you will not see pictures or hear sounds on the screen unless you download them and have the appropriate software to activate them. The only thing you will see is the textual information (which is the most important). Text browsers work very much like Gopher menus.

Accessing the World Wide Web

To access the WWW, use the menu on your system, or type "**WWW**" or "**Web**". One of these methods should give you access to the WWW. If not, consult with your sysop or your local computer center.

The WWW works much like Gopher in that you do not have to download documents to read them. You can read them right on the screen and decide whether or not you want to download them. The Web also includes hypertext, which allows documents to be connected to one another. The way it works is that in each document you read, there will be words that are highlighted words. As you read the document, you can place the cursor on the highlighted word, press the Enter key, and access another document that it is connected to without knowing its exact WWW address. For example, if you are reading a document about applying to graduate schools, each school's name may be highlighted. If you put the cursor on that word and press Enter, you will go to another WWW site that contains another document about the highlighted word. In this way, documents are interconnected. They may also be connected with pictures and sounds.

When you log onto the WWW, you will go onto your access provider's home page. Web sites are also called *web pages*. Most universities have their own pages, which they call their home pages. Much like Gopher servers, these home pages will act like a menu system that will take you to documents related to the university or to other WWW sites.

About URL Addresses

If you want to jump directly to a web page that you know the address of, you have to know the command for your browser to access another page. There should be directions somewhere on your screen, or type "**help**". Text browsers often work by typing "**go {URL}**", where URL (pronounced *earl*) is the WWW address. Graphical browsers usually have a rectangular box at the top of the screen where you type in the address. It should not be difficult to figure out, but if you have trouble, contact your sysop. As you can see, WWW addresses have a special name. They are called *URLs*, or *Universal Resource Locators*. Every site on the Internet has its own URL or address. Here are three examples of what URLs look like:

http://rdz.stjohns.edu/~warren/psych.html
ftp://wuarchive.wustl.edu/mirrors
news:alt.psychology

The first part of the URL, to the left of the colon, tells you how the browser will access that particular site. For example, when accessing a newsgroup URL, the address starts with news. Here is a list of the most common access methods:

ftp	File Transfer Protocol
file	File Transfer Protocol
news	Usenet newsgroup
gopher	Gopher
http	Hypertext Transport Protocol

By now you should be familiar with some of these terms. When you see an URL with http at the beginning, this means that you are accessing a hypertext document. The rest of the URL, the part to the right of the colon, is the is the address of the particular site along with the subdirectory. The sub-directory is the area on the computer that you are accessing where the information you are looking for is kept.

Search Engines

An invaluable tool to use on the WWW is a *search engine*. Search engines are WWW pages where you can search for information by simply typing in one or two key words. For example, if you were interested in information about Pavlov, you would go to a search engine and type in **"Pavlov"** in the appropriate place. All the available information about Pavlov will then appear. One search engine that you can try is:

>   **http://www.infoseek.com**

When you go to this site, you will see a blank line that looks like this:

_____

Type in the term that you would like to search for, and then go to the word search that is highlighted and press Enter. You will soon get pages and pages of the results of your search.

Downloading and Viruses

Downloading from the WWW is the same as from Gopher. Just find out what command your browser uses to download and use it. If you are downloading program files (computer software), read Chapter 9 for the instructions.

Don't worry about contracting viruses by surfing the Web except if you download a program file. Any program files that you download from the Internet should be checked for viruses.

Table 8.1 lists World Wide Web URLs.

Internet Activities

1. Find out what type of Web browser you have access to.

2. If you don't have a graphical browser, speak to your sysop and see if it is possible to get one for your account.

3. Log onto and explore the WWW.

4. Learn which command your browser uses to go directly to URLs and use it.

"Clinical and Psychology" Search Results
http://galaxy.einet.net/galaxy/Social-Sciences/Psychology/Clinical.html

"Psychiatry" Search Results
http://galaxy.einet.net/galaxy/Medicine/Medical-Specialties/
Psychiatry/search-results.html#WWW

A resource page for psychologists early in their careers
http://tigger.oslc.org/Ecpn/intro.html

ABUSE/RECOVERY INFORMATION Dissociation and
sexual abuse recovery FAQ
http://www.tezcat.com/~tina/psych.html

AL-Anon and ALATEEN WWW site
http://solar.rtd.utk.edu/~al-anon/

Alzheimer Web
http://werple.mira.net.au/~dhs/ad.html

American Psychological Association
http://matia.stanford.edu/cogsci/org.html#apa
http://www.apa.org/

American Academy of Child and Adolescent Psychiatry
http://www.med.umich.edu/aacap/homepage.html

A listing of American universities
http://www.clas.ufl.edu/CLAS/american-universities.html

Annual meeting information—Cognitive Science Society
http://info.pitt.edu/~cogsci95/

Anxiety and Panic Attacks
http://www.hslib.washington.edu/hsc/newsinfo/healthbeat/panic.html

Attention Deficit Disorder WWW Archives
http://www.seas.upenn.edu/~mengwong/add/
http://www.seas.upenn.edu:80/~mengwong/add/
http://www.seas.upenn.edu/~mengwong/add/add.faq.html

ATTENTION-DEFICIT DISORDER Jasper-Goldberg Adult ADD Screening
Examination, Version 5.0
http://www.ucar.edu/pendulum/cows.html

Australian National University Social Services Library
http://coombs.anu.edu.au/WWWVL-SocSci.html
http://coombs.anu.edu.au/CoombsHome.html

Autism Help Line
http://fiona.umsmed.edu/-sturges/autism.text

AUTISM FAQ by John Wobus
http://web.syr.edu/~jmwobus/autism/autism.faq

Behavior Analysis List Server Information
http://www.coedu.usf.edu/behavior/listserv.html

BIOFEEDBACK/NEUROFEEDBACK/NEUROSCIENCE Neurosciences
http://ivory.lm.com:80/~nab/

BIOMED and PSYCHLINKS
http://www.cris.com/~lkarper/hotlists.html#Biomed

BIPOLAR DISORDERS
http://www.ucar.edu/pendulum/
http://www.ucar.edu/pendulum/index.html

Blain Nelson's Domestic Violence/Abuse page
http://www.wwu.edu/~n9348795/dv/

Center for Anxiety and Stress Treatment
http://www.cts.com/~health/

Child Behavior Checklist (Achenbach CBCL)
gopher://moose.uvm.edu:70/11/Other%20UVM%20Gophers%20and%20
Information%20Resources/University%20Associates%20in%20Psychiatry/Child
%20Behavior%20Checklist%20%28Achenbach%20CBCL%29 (one word)

Cocaine Anonymous Information
http://www.ca.org/infoline.html

Cognitive Psychology and Psychology Lynx or Mosaic connection to:
http://mambo.ucsc.edu/psl/psych.html
http://www.gatech.edu
http://beowulf.uwaterloo.ca
http://www.cc.gatech.edu/cogsci/cogsci.html
http://www.lifesci.ucla.edu
http://www.cogs.susx.ac.uk
http://matia.stanford.edu/cogsci/

Cognitive Science Server Lynx or Mosaic connection to:
http://www.psych.indiana.edu

Cognitive and Psychological Sciences on the Internet
http://matia.stanford.edu/cogsci/

Cognitive Science Internet Resources—Brown University, Rhode Island
http://www.cog.brown.edu/pointers/cognitive.html

COGNITIVE PSYCHOLOGY Indiana University Cognitive Science
http://www.psych.indiana.edu/

Counseling Center, State University of New York at Buffalo
ftp://ftp.cs.monash.edu.au/psyche/psyche-95-2-5-qm_stapp-1-stapp.txt

CounselorNet SUNY/ Plattsburgh.
gopher://baryon.hawk.plattsburgh.edu 70.

CTI Centre for Psychology News
http://ctipsych.york.ac.uk/ctipsych.html

Depression FAQ
fttp://avocado.pc.helsinki.fi/~janne/asdfaq/index.html

Depression FAQ from USENET alt.support.depression
ftp://rtfm.mit.edu/pub/usenet/alt.support.depression/

Domestic Abuse
http://www.tezcat.com/~tina/psych.html

Dr. Bob's Home Page—Medical/Mental Health Resources
http://uhs.bsd.uchicago.edu/~bhsiung/mental.html

Drug-related network resources
http://hyperreal.com/drugs/faqs/resources.html
http://www.pitt.edu/~mbtst3/druginfo.html
http://www.pitt.edu/~mbtst3/druginfo.html#WWW SITES

E-Mail discussion groups
http://alpha.acast.nova.edu/listserv.html

Eating Disorders
http://ccwf.cc.utexas.edu/~bjackson/UTHealth/eating.html

Electronic Journal of Behavior Analysis and Therapy
http://rs1.cc.und.nodak.edu/misc/jBAT/jbatinfo.html

Emotional Trauma Info Pages
The "Trauma Info Pages" include 5 pages (topics) of information. There
is some narrative text about traumatic-stress; trauma resources on the
web that can be read, joined, or searched; links to general supportive
information; disaster mental health handouts I've collected or been
given; and web links to other interesting sites (most but not all of
which have something to do with traumatic stress or disasters,
psychology, neuroscience, etc.).
http://gladstone.uoregon.edu/~dvb/trauma.htm

General hospital—Mental health and society by Margaret Crane/Jon Winet
http://pubweb.parc.xerox.com/hypertext/pair/cw/gh.html

Gopher Jewels on Psychology
http://galaxy.einet.net/GJ/psychology.html

Habit Smart http://www.cts.com:80/~habtsmrt/

Hanover College Home Page
An ambitious and impressive list of Internet sites related to psychology created
by Dr. John H. Krantz
http://psych.hanover.edu

Huge database from the Texas State Electronic Library
gopher://jennie.tsl.texas gov:70/11/.dir/sjmental.dir

Hypnosis
http://www.utu.fi/~jounsmed/asc/hyp.html

Hypnosis and NLP by Lee Lady
ftp://ftp.hawaii.edu/outgoing/lady/

IEC ProGAMMA: The Social Science Information Technology Server
http://www.gamma.rug.nl/

Internet Resources for Physical Loss, Chronic Illness, and Bereavement
http://asa.ugl.lib.umich.edu/chdocs/support/emotion.html

InterPsych conference list
http://www.med.umich.edu/psychiatry/interpsych.html

Ivan Goldberg's Home Page—Psychiatry and Depression
http://avocado.pc.helsinki.fi/~janne/ikg/

JOSEPH PLAUD WWW site:
He has been working on a home page that is comprehensive as a psychology
resource, among other things. This page is located at the University of North
Dakota and has a behavioral/experimental orientation.
http://rs1.cc.und.nodak.edu/misc/JBAT/

Journal of the Experimental Analysis of Behavior
http://www.envmed.rochester.edu/wwwrap/behavior/jeab/jeabhome.htm

Journal of Applied Behavior Analysis
http://www.envmed.rochester.edu/wwwrap/behavior/jaba/jabahome.htm

Journal of Constructivist Psychology
http://ksi.cpsc.ucalgary.ca/PCP/JCP95.html

Med Web
http://www.cc.emory.edu/WHSCL/medweb.mentalhealth.html

Medical Newsgroups http://world-health.net/newsgrou.html

Medical List by Jeanine Wade, Ph.D., Licensed Psychologist, Austin, Texas
http://www.realtime.net/~mmjw/

Medical Health Publishing
http://world-health.net/

Men, Rape, and Sexual Assault
http://www.vix.com/pub/men/abuse/abuse.html

Men and Domestic Violence Index
http://www.vix.com/pub/men/domestic-index.html

Mental Health Policy Information Exchange
http://www.pie.org/

Mental Illness in General Health Care: An International Study
http://www.who.ch/

Mental Health Links by Chris Wolfe
http://miavx1.muohio.edu/~crwolfe/mental_health.html

Metuchen Psychological Services
http://www.castle.net/~tbogen/mps.html

Myers Briggs type test online
http://sunsite.unc.edu/personality/keirsey.html

Mind Media—free software, great links, self-improvement, and creativity
http://www.mindmedia.com

Mood Disorders
http://avocado.pc.helsinki.fi/~janne/mood/mood.html
http://avocado.pc.helsinki.fi/~janne/asdfaq/

Mood Disorders
http://hakatai.mcli.dist.maricopa.edu/smc/ml/mood-server.html

National Institute of Mental Health—Stigma of Mental Illness
gopher://gopher.gsa.gov:70/00/staff/pa/cic/health/stigma

Newsletter of the Society for I/O Psychology
http://cmit.unomaha.edu/tip/tip/html

Neural Processes in Cognition
HTTP://neurocog.lrdc.pitt.edu:80/npc/

Neuro-Linguistic Programming and Design Human Engineering
http://www.nlp.com/NLP/

Neurofeedback Archive
http://www.primenet.com/~thielbl/neuroarc.html

Neuroscience Internet Resource Guide
http://http2.sils.umich.edu/Public/nirg/nirg1.html

New WWW project for LISTSERV lists
http://tile.net/listserv/

Normal personality archive (alt.psychology.personality)
http://sunsite.unc.edu/personality/

Nova Southeastern University
http://alpha.acast.nova.edu/health/psy/psy.html

Obsessive Compulsive Disorder Home Page
http://mtech.csd.uwm.edu/~fairlite/ocd.html

Personality Type Summary (Myers-Briggs)
http://www.ucar.edu/pendulum/MB.html

Public Broadcasting System (PBS)
http://www.pbs.org

Practical Psychology Magazine
http://www.thegroup.net/ppm/ppmhome.htm

Processes in Cognition
http://neurocog.lrdc.pitt.edu/npc/

PsycGrad WWW Site
This site connects to newsgroups related to psychology.
http://www.cc.utexas.edu/psycgrad

PSYCH WEB
This is a web site for students and teachers of psychology. There are loads of
links, plus an accumulation of useful documents for students and teachers of
psychology, and some interesting feature articles from past issues of the
departmental newsletter.
http://www.gasou.edu/psychweb/psychweb.htm

Psyche (On consciousness)
http://hcrl.open.ac.uk/psyche.html

Psychiatry Star (New WWW Site at University of Michigan)
http://www.psych.med.umich.edu/

PSYCHIATRY ON LINE
http://www.cityscape.co.uk/users/ad88/psych.htm

PsychLink
http://www.psychiatry.pitt.edu/

Psychology from EINet Galaxy
http://www.einet.net/galaxy/Social-Sciences/Psychology.html

Psychology Sites Worldwide by sturges@fiona.umsmed.edu
http://fiona.umsmed.edu/~sturges/psych.html

Psychology Around The World Home Page
http://rs1.cc.und.nodak.edu/misc/JBAT/psychres.html

Psychology Electronic Journals
http://psych.hanover.edu/Krantz/journal.html

Psychology and Psychiatry
http://www.clark.net/pub/lschank/web/behave.html

Psychology and Support Groups Newsgroup Pointer—John M. Grohol
file://rtfm.mit.edu/pub/usenet/alt.abuse.transcendence/Psychology_&
_Support_Groups_Newsgroup_Pointer (one word)

PSYCHOLOGY WEB POINTER
http://www.tezcat.com/~tina/psych.pages/grohol.web-pointers.html

Psychopharmacology and Substance Abuse WWW Page
http://charlotte.med.nyu.edu/woodr/div28.html

Psychopharmacology Tips
http://uhs.bsd.uchicago.edu/~bhsiung/tips.html

Psycoloquy can be accessed in many ways
http://cogsci.ecs.soton.ac.uk/~harnad/psyc.html
http://www.princeton.edu/~harnad/psyc.html
gopher://gopher.princeton.edu:70/11/.libraries/.pujournals
ftp://ftp.princeton.edu/pub/harnad/
ftp://cogsci.ecs.soton.ac.uk/pub/harnad
news:sci.psychology.journals.psycoloquy

PTSD general information
http://www.long-beach.va.gov/ptsd/stress.html

PTSD/combat veterans research
http://141.163.90.14/intro.htm

Qualitative Research and Analysis Server Lynx or Mosaic connection to:
http://qsr.latrobe.edu.au/Public/WWW/resources.html

RESEARCH INFO
http://superior.carlton.ca/~szikopou/methods.html

Safety Net: Domestic Violence Resources
http://www.interport.net/~asherman/dv.html

Science: Psychology
http://www.yahoo.com/Science/Psychology

Self-Help Psychology Magazine home page
http://www.well.com:80/www/selfhelp/index.html
http://www.well.com/www/selfhelp

SELF-HELP PSYCHOLOGY MAGAZINE
http://www.well.com/www/selfhelp

Serotonin article
http://mtech.csd.uwm.edu/~fairlite/ocd/ser90.html

Sexual Assault Information Page
http://www.cs.utk.edu/~bartley/saInfoPage.html

Sexual Disorders Page
http://www.cityscape.co.uk/users/ad88/sex.htm

Sleep Centers on the Web
http://www.hooked.net/users/tompace/sdc.html

SleepNet
http://www.sleepnet.com/

Social Sciences Information Gateway—United Kingdom
http://sosig.esrc.bris.ac.uk:80/

Social Cognition: Stereotypes in Mass Media and Society
This is a resource for those in education circles or anyone interested in waking
up to the world around us. It is an informative and interesting look at cultures
other than (and in most cases including) your own.
http://fire.clarkson.edu/~rizzojp/proj.html

Society for Computers in Psychology
http://www.lafayette.edu/allanr/scip.html

Society of Industrial/Organizational Psychology web page
http://cmit.unomaha.edu/TIP/TIP.html

Sociology and Psychology Resources on the Internet
http://darkwing.uoregon.edu/~huayi/SOCPSY.HTML

Spirit-WWW New Age web site, articles on Healing and Spiritual Crisis
http://spirit.satelnet.org/Spirit/blais.html

Statistical help, health, psychopharmacology
http://superior.carleton.ca/~szikopou/

Statistical and data analysis software (shareware)
http://www.compulink.co.uk/kovcomp/

Statistics Server Lynx or Mosaic connection to:
http//www.stat.washington.edu/index.html

Steven Harnad's Home Page
http://cogsci.soton.ac.uk/~harnad/

Subject Specific Resource List in Psychology
gopher://ukoln.bath.ac.uk:7070/00/Link/Tree/Psychology/1501_-_Subject
_Specific_Resource_List_in_Psychology (one word)

The North American Psycoloquy Archive
http://www.princeton.edu/~harnad/psyc.html

The Option Institute
http://www.human.com/mkt/option

The Florida Mental Health Institute University of South Florida, Tampa
http://www.fmhi.usf.edu/

The Sleep Medicine Home Page
http://www.cloud9.net:80/~thorpy/

The APA has a Web page
http://www.apa.org

The Society for Computers in Psychology (SCiP)
http://www.lafayette.edu/allanr/scip.html

The Awesome list by John S. Makulowich
http://www.clark.net/pub/journalism/awesome.html

The Psychopharmacology Tips Web Page
http://uhs.bsd.uchicago.edu/~bhsiung/tips.html

The GROHOL Mental Health Page
http://www1.mhv.net/~grohol

The Wolfeman's Hot Links
http://miavx1.muohio.cdu/~crwolfc/hot_links.html

This Web Pointer
http://www.gold.net/users/ck51/www/psychology.html

Tim Smith, University of Pittsburgh, Learning Research and
Development Center
http://neurocog.lrdc.pitt.edu/~tws

Tom Scholberg's Home Page—Grohol's Newsgroups Pointer
http://chat.carleton.ca/~tscholbe/
http://chat.carleton.ca/~tscholbe/psych.html

Trauma and Dissociation
http://www.access.digex.net/~sidran/

Trauma
http://gladstone.uoregon.edu/~dvb/trauma.htm

University of California, San Diego (UCSD), Psychology Deptartment
http://psy.ucsd.edu/

University of Michigan Psychiatry Home Page
http://www.med.umich.edu/psychiatry/homepage.html

University of Leicester, U.K.—Division of Child Psychiatry
http://www.le.ac.uk/CWIS/AD/GWINST/greenwood.html

UNIVERSITY OF MISSISSIPPI Medical Center Psychology internship sites
http://fiona.umsmed.edu/~sturges/brochure

UNIVERSITY OF MARYLAND AT COLLEGE PARK Counseling Center
http://www.inform.umd.edu/Student_Information_And_Resources/
Counseling_Health_Services (one word)

VIRGINIA TECH University Counseling Center
http://www.ucc.vt.edu

WARREN BUSH'S PSYCHOLOGY CYBER SYNAPSE
http://rdz.stjohns.edu/~warren/psych.html

Washington University Human Brain Project
http://www1.biostr.washington.edu/BrainProject.html

Welcome to The Arc's World Wide Web Site
http://fohnix.metronet.com/~thearc/welcome.html

Western Psychiatric Institute and Clinic
http://www.pitt.edu/~wplib/
http://www.pitt.edu/~wplib/psychiatry.html

William H. Calvin's Home Page - Neurophysiologist
http://weber.u.washington.edu/wcalvin/

Winter Depression (SAD) Information
http://www.ucar.edu/pendulum/sad.html

YAHOO
This is a comprehensive psychology site.
http://www.yahoo.com/social_science

CHAPTER 9: FILE TRANSFER PROTOCOL

What Is File Transfer Protocol?

File Transfer Protocol (*FTP*) is an Internet application program that is used to download, or transfer, software programs and *text files* from the Internet to your computer. Just like e-mail, where you can send letters from one computer to another, FTP allows any type of computer file to be sent from one computer to another. In this way, you can transfer software, or even large files that contain as much information as an encyclopedia, over the Internet. These files are kept at places called *FTP sites*. The Internet has many FTP sites that contain, in computer file form, journal articles and books about psychology that can be downloaded. There are also many sites that contain software programs that can be used to write testing reports and measure psychological variables such as reaction time. These sites are actually computers on the Internet that store computer files for public access. You can use the FTP program to download files from FTP sites.

Accessing FTP

1. To access FTP, as with the other Internet applications, first see if your menu system has a command for FTP. If not, type "**FTP**" at the prompt. There are many different FTP access programs, so each one may have different commands (see Table 9.1). If you can't figure out how to access FTP, contact your sysop.

2. To access an FTP site, you need to know the address. FTP addresses generally look something like this:

   ftp.iupui.edu/pub/pc/psychiat

   The address includes the FTP site address and *subdirectory* that you will have to access in order to find the file you want. In the example, ftp.iupui.edu is the FTP address. Everything to the right of the first / is the subdirectory that the file is in. A subdirectory is an organizing system used on computers to separate files by category. For example, in a /pub/pc/psychiat subdirectory, you might find files related to psychiatry. In this example, the file you want is in the /pub/pc/psychiat subdirectory.

Table 9.1   FTP COMMANDS

OPEN {FTP address}	Go to FTP address.
GET {filename}	Download file. Filename has to be written exactly as it is on the FTP directory (capitals must be capitals, and lower-case letters must be lower-case letters).
TYPE {binary} or {text}	Change download type to binary or text depending on which type of file you are downloading. Programs are always binary files. Most others are text.
DIR or LS	List files on the current directory. One of these commands will work.
CD /{subdirectory}	Change directory to subdirectory of choice.
CLOSE or QUIT	Logoff of an FTP site.

Going to an FTP Site

1. The command to go to an FTP site is **"open {ftp address}"**. Using the preceding FTP address as an example, you would type **"open ftp.iupui.edu"** and press Enter. You will then have to wait while it gains access to the site. The best time to access FTP sites is after business hours. All the sites that we will use in this manual are *anonymous FTP sites*, which allow you to logon and download files without an account at that particular site.

2. When you are connected to the FTP site, it will ask you for a password. Type in **"anonymous"** or whatever password they suggest you use. Anonymous is a universal password that will give you limited access to any anonymous FTP site.

3. You will then be asked for an ID. Type in your full e-mail address or whatever else they request. This is done so that the FTP sysop can keep track of how many persons logon to a particular FTP site.

4. You will next see a list of subdirectories and files. If you don't see such a list, type **"DIR"** or **"LS"**, and a list of files should appear.

Downloading Index Files

1. Look down the list for a file named index.txt or something similar. Almost all FTP sites will have an index file. The first thing you should

do is download the index file, which will tell you what is available at that site. You cannot read the index file on the FTP site itself.

2. To download an index file, type **"get filename"**, where filename is the exact name, including periods and dashes, of the index file you want to download. The get command is *case sensitive*, so you have to type the filename exactly as it appears on your screen. For example, if the index file is in all capital letters, you have to type **"get INDEX"**.

3. You will then be asked to give the file a name so that it can be saved on your local directory. Give the file a name that you will remember, preferably, index. Press Enter, or follow the instructions on the screen to begin downloading.

4. You will now see the file downloading. There is usually a timer that will tell you how much of the file has downloaded and how long it will take to complete the download. It usually takes less than one minute to download a file from an FTP site.

5. After it has downloaded, type **"quit"** or **"exit"**. One of these commands should return you to your local system.

6. Now type **"close"**, or follow the menu commands of your system to get to your main directory.

7. You will now be back on your own Internet account. Type **"DIR"** or **"LS"** or whatever the command on your system is to see all the files. You should see a list of files on your directory, including the index file that you just downloaded.

Text Files and Binary Files

The file is now on your account directory. You can read it there or download it to your computer or floppy disk and read it using any word processor. Look through the index file for the names of any text files or program files that you may be interested in. If you find a file that you think might be interesting to look at, you will have to know two things: the complete address (including the subdirectory that it is in) and the *file type* (either text or *binary*). Text files, also called ASCII files, contain words only, such as the index file that you downloaded. (All index files are text files.) Binary files contain computer software programs. They are called binary files because they are stored as 1's and 0's, which is called binary form. Text files can be downloaded the same way that you downloaded the index file. Program files have to be downloaded as binary files so that when you download them you do not distort them. Instructions on how to change the file type follow.

If you decide that you would like to download a file, write down the full address and filename. Follow the instructions at the beginning of the chapter to log back on to the FTP site. Remember, logging on at night is usually better.

1. After you log back on, you will have to go to the subdirectory where the file is located. The subdirectory is the part of the address after the /. You will have to change to that subdirectory.

2. To change directories, type "**cd /directory**", where directory is the exact name of the directory in the address you have. Notice that there is a space between the cd and the /. Using the earlier example, once you've logged on, you would type "**cd /pub/pc/psychiat**". This would then bring you to that subdirectory where the file you want is located.

3. Now type "**DIR**" or "**LS**" to see a list of the files available in that subdirectory. Your file should be there. If it is not, either you were given the wrong address or the file is no longer there. Remember, the Internet is very chaotic; files that are there one day may be gone the next day. If you wish to download a text file, you can follow the instructions you used to download the index file.

4. To download a binary file, type "**type binary**". This will change the file type to binary, and you can now download software programs using the "**get filename**" command. The program will now download onto your local directory.

5. To use program files, you have to download them again to a disk or to your own computer. When you download programs to a floppy disk or your computer, you have to download them again as binary files. Since many different communications programs are used to download from your local account, you will have to contact your local sysop to find out how to change the file type to binary in order to download the program to your computer or floppy disk. If your download program has a menu, find the option for changing it to binary and use it. The program can then be downloaded onto a disk or your computer.

Decompressing Files

Most program files will have .zip as their extension (for example, program.zip). This means that the file is compressed so that it takes up less disk space and can be downloaded faster. To decompress it, you will need a copy of Pkunzip™. Pkunzip™ is a compression/decompression program that is used to decompress the files. Pkunzip™ can be accessed on FTP sites.

You will need a copy of Pkunzip™ if you want to download and use program files.

When you have a copy of Pkunzip™ (instructions to get a copy follow), type "**pkunzip {name of zip file}**" or "**unzip {name of zip file}**" (there are different versions of this program, but one of these commands will work), where the name of the zip file is the file that you downloaded from the FTP site. The file will now decompress and be ready for use. There will usually be a file called *read.me* after you decompress the zip file. You can read the read.me file using any word processor or text editor. This file will give you instructions on how to install and use the program.

Shareware and Freeware

Programs that you download from the Internet usually consist of two types, shareware and freeware. Shareware programs are programs that you are allowed to copy and distribute to others. For example, many games on the Internet are shareware programs. Usually, you are allowed to use the program for 30 days for no fee. If you like the program, and plan to continue to use it, you should send in the requested fee. If you don't, nothing terrible will happen to you or your computer, and the program will continue to work. It's just more courteous to send in the fee, and usually you will be sent any upgrades for free.

Freeware, on the other hand, is free without limitations. For example, Netscape™, a program that is used heavily on the Internet, is freeware. You can use these programs, copy them, and distribute them for no charge. The status of freeware programs can change often, and some organizations are required to purchase freeware. Netscape™ is available for free for individual users, but companies must pay a licensing fee to use it. Please check the status of each program before you use it.

Archie

Archie is an application available on most Internet accounts that is used to search for programs and text files on anonymous FTP sites. To use archie, see if you can access it through a menu system, or type "**archie**". You will then be asked to give archie the name of the file that you want. You must type in the name exactly as it would appear on the FTP site. Usually, program names are not in capital letters. The first program you will need is Pkunzip™, so let's try to find that file. Using archie, you can search for "**unzip.exe**". Depending on which archie program you have, either you will be told immediately where this program can be accessed or you will be sent the information via e-mail. Each archie program works differently. After you have the address for unzip.exe, you can use FTP to get to that site and download it. Remember, you must download it as a binary file since

Pkunzip™ is a software program. Once you download it to your account, you have to download it to a disk or your own computer as a binary file. Once it is downloaded to a disk or a computer, it is ready to use.

Viruses from FTP Sites

Downloading programs from FTP sites is an easy way to contract viruses on your computer even though FTP sysops usually check for them before a program is posted. Viruses usually hide in files with an .exe or .com extension in their name. Before you run any program that you download from an FTP site, run it through a virus program to check for viruses. You should be able to get a virus cleaning program from your sysop.

Table 9.2 lists FTP site addresses. (Remember, FTP sites come and go. Some of these sites may no longer exist.)

Internet Activities

1. Find out the command for your system for accessing FTP.

2. Logon to several anonymous FTP sites, and download the index files. Read through these files for any program or document that you are interested in. Download the files of programs that you want.

3. Run the program files through a virus program. If they contain no viruses, you will be ready to decompress them using Pkunzip™.

4. Use archie to find an address for the unzip.exe file that you will need to decompress program files.

5. Logon to the anonymous FTP site, and download unzip.exe. Remember, since this is a program file, you must download it as a binary file. Download the file, again, to a disk or your computer.

6. Using Pkunzip™, decompress the program file.

7. Your program files are now ready to be used. Find the file named read.me, and read it with any word processor. This file will give you instructions on how to use the program or programs you have downloaded.

Table 9.2   FTP SITE ADDRESSES

Depression FAQ from USENET alt.support.depression
ftp://rtfm.mit.edu/pub/usenet/alt.support.depression/

Hypnosis and NLP by Lee Lady
ftp://ftp.hawaii.edu/outgoing/lady/

FTP Site for Mental Health Programs
ftp.iupui.edu/pub/pc/psychiat

Lee Hancock's Health Resources Guide
file://ftp.sura.net/pub/nic/medical.resources.9-93)

Neuropsych FTP Site. Everything you ever wanted to know about neuropsych.
Ftp.una.hh.lib.umich.edu/inetdirsstacks//neurosci:cormbonaria

ETS Test Locator
Ftp: rigel.acs.oakland.edu/pub/msdos/

Ftp: wuarchive.wustl.edu/mirrors/msdos/

Ftp: msdos.archive.umich.edu

Ftp: cica.indiana.edu/pub/pc/borland or win3

Ftp: archive.orst.edu

Ftp: bode.ee.ualberta.ca

Ftp: m-media.muohio.edu

National software archive, Lancaster University (HENSA), UK.
Ftp: micros.hensa.ac.uk
Use 'hensa' for username and password.

COMPsych. This is an electronic software information service and PC software
archive for psychology.
FTP: GLUON.HAWK.PLATTSBURGH.EDU/pub/compsych

NLP (NeuroLinguistic Programming)
FTP: ftp.hawaii.edu/outgoing/lady

Charles Tart's archive
FTP: ftp.ucdavis.edu/pub/fztart

Medical Resources List
FTP: FTP.SURA.NET/pub/nic

Centre for Cognitive Sciences
FTP: scott.cogsci.ed.ac.uk

The SPSS FTP site
ftp.spss.com, so from
This site contains many statistical software packages as well as articles about
statistics.

CHAPTER 10: APA REFERENCE STYLE FOR INTERNET RESOURCES

Guidelines on How to Cite On-Line Information

The fourth edition of the APA (American Psychological Association) Publication Manual states that there is no standard set yet for on-line information, but there are some guidelines to follow. The purpose of a reference is to credit the author and enable the reader to access the information, so make an effort to include this information. At this point, enabling the reader to access the information may be difficult because, as you know, Internet sites come and go. If a printed copy of the reference exists, give the printed source's information so that others can access that. If not, follow the APA reference guidelines.

APA Reference Guidelines

> Author, I. (date). Title of article. *Name of Periodical* [on-line], *xx*.
> Available: Address on the Internet.

"Author" is the author's last name.
"I" is the author's middle and first initials.
"(date)" is the date that the source was written or last updated.
"*xx*" is the edition number (if applicable).
"Address on the Internet" should be the exact address where the source is located. If the source has been archived, give the archive address. If the source is an on-line journal, give the server address for the journal and the command necessary to access that article. Many journals are archived on Gopher and WWW sites, so that address may be easier for others to access. Always give the full address, including passwords, if necessary, and subdirectories.

Here is an example:

> Mahony, D. (Ed). (1995). *Psychology Internet Resource list* [on-line], 3A.
> Available: http://rdz.stjohns.edu /~warren/psych.html

This is a new way to access information, so give the reader as much information as you can.

You may also want to reference personal communications (e-mail) that you receive from others on the Internet. Since personal communication is not available to others, you cite it in the text only, for example, D. Mahony (personal communication, May 23, 1995). Be as precise as you can about the date.

HELPFUL REFERENCES

American Psychological Association. 1994. *Publication Manual of the American Psychological Association* (4th ed.). Washington, D.C.: American Psychological Association.

Crispin, P., D. (1994). *Roadmap* [on-line].
    Available e-mail: listserv@ua1vm.ua.edu
    Message: get week{1-6} package f=mail

Griffin, A. (1993). *EFF's Guide to the Internet* or *Big Dummies Guide to the Internet* (v.3.1). Washington, D.C.: The Electronic Frontier Foundation.

Mahony, D. (1995). *Psychology Internet Resource List* [on-line], (3A). Available: http://rdz.stjohns.edu/~warren/psych.html

GLOSSARY

Abstract   Overview of a research article. It will include the hypothesis, the methods, the subjects, and the results of the study.

Account Directory   Directory on your host's system where your files are kept.

Address   The alphanumeric code that will get you to a particular Internet site or to a user's e-mail box, for example, http://www/apa.org. This is the WWW address for the American Psychological Association.

Address Book   Computer file that keeps all the e-mail addresses that you use so that you do not have to type out long addresses each time you send an e-mail.

Address Field   Space in e-mail program where you type in the e-mail address that you want to send to.

Anonymous FTP Site   FTP site that allows you to logon and download files without an account at that site.

Archie   Program that will search for computer files on the Internet for you.

Browser   Program that is used to access the World Wide Web, for example, Netscape or Mosaic.

BTW   By the way.

Byte   Unit of measurement for disk space.

Cancel Command   Command that is used to cancel the Internet application that you are running. This command is used when you get stuck.

Case Sensitive   Means that the command has to be typed exactly as specified. Don't use capital letters in place of lower-case letters and vice versa.

Communications Software   Software that enables you to connect to your Internet account from your PC at home.

Database   Compilation of data, such as PsycLit™, which compiles all psychological journal abstracts.

Directory   Subgrouping of files on a computer. Directories are used to keep computer files organized by separating them by some category.

Discussion Address   Address where e-mail is sent that you want all other readers to see.

Domain Name   Address of a computer that is connected to the Internet.

Down   Refers to a computer that is not working for some reason, for example, the system is down. It will usually be fixed within a short time.

Download   To transfer documents or software from your Internet access account to your home computer or floppy disk.

E-Mail   Electronic mail. This is the most basic feature of an Internet account that allows you to send letters electronically to any other person with an e-mail account.

E-Mail Address   Alphanumeric characters that are used to address an e-mail. Each individual has his or her own unique e-mail address.

E-Mail Discussion Group   List of subscribers that send e-mail back and forth regarding a certain topic.

FAQ   Frequently Asked Questions. Document that answers common questions regarding a Usenet newsgroup, discussion group, FTP, Gopher, or WWW site.

File Type   Binary or text. Binary files are usually software files that will execute a program. They are stored in binary form, or 1's and 0's. Text or ASCII files have text (writing) in them.

Flame   To disagree with another Internet user in an unpolite way.

Floppy Disk   5¼- or 3½-inch computer disk that is inserted into a computer to transfer data.

FTP   File Transfer Protocol. This is a program that allows you to download documents and software from FTP sites.

FTP Sites   Computers all over the world that allow you to download software and documents for no charge.

Freeze   Images on the screen do not respond to the keyboard commands. You need to use the cancel command at this point.

Gopher   An Internet access program that allows you to navigate the Internet by following a menu system.

Gopherspace   Interconnected Gopher sites.

Hacker   Individual that breaks into computers illegally to copy software or gain access to privileged information.

Hard Copy   Copy of a document on paper as opposed to on a computer file.

Hard Drive   Place on computer where files are stored magnetically.

HTTP   Hypertext Transport Protocol.

Hypertext   Documents that are linked so that when you go to a highlighted word in one document and press Enter, you will go to another document.

IMHO   In my humble opinion.

Inbox   Place in e-mail program where incoming e-mail is kept.

Internet   A system of computers that are connected to one another by phone lines. It consists, primarily, of government and university computers all over the world.

Internet Access Account   An account at a local Internet provider that allows you to access the Internet.

Internet Application Program   Computer program that allows you to communicate with others and search for information on the Internet, for example, WWW and Gopher.

IP Address   Address of a computer connected to the Internet.

Join   To sign up to an e-mail discussion group.

Kermit   Communications software and downloading protocol.

Listen In   To lurk.

Listproc   E-mail discussion group server.

Lists   Discussion groups.

Listserv   Popular e-mail discussion group server.

Listserver   Programs that are used to execute commands and send e-mail for discussion groups, for example, Listserv, Majordomo, and Listproc.

Listserver Address   Address of a listserver where all commands are sent.

Logon   To connect to the Internet with a computer.

Logon Procedure   Set of commands needed to access your Internet account. This includes the phone number to your account, password, and ID number.

Lurk   To read e-mail from a discussion group without responding.

Mailbase   E-mail discussion group server.

Mailer-Daemon   This is an Internet program that will return your e-mail to you if the address is incorrect or if your e-mail is undeliverable for some reason.

Mail Received Folder   Place in e-mail program where incoming e-mail is kept.

Mail Server   Computer that sends and receives e-mail for Internet accounts.

Menu   Options that are available to guide you at a particular Internet site. To activate a menu option, place the cursor on it and press Enter.

Menu-Driven System   Options that are available to you at a particular Internet site. To activate a menu option, place the cursor on the item of interest and press Enter. You will then go to other menus until you reach what you are looking for.

Modem   Device that you connect to your computer that will connect it to a phone line.

Netiquette   Etiquette when you are on the Internet. Each Internet forum has its own netiquette.

On-Line Journals   Journals that are published on the Internet. These journals are sent to subscribers by e-mail and kept at FTP, Gopher, and WWW sites.

Password   Alphanumeric code that allows only you to access your Internet account.

Peer Review   Research results are reviewed by other experts in the field for accuracy and criticism.

PPP Connection   Special connection to the Internet that allows you to use graphical WWW browsers.

Program File   Computer file that contains software as opposed to plain text.

PsycLit™   Database of abstracts of psychology journal articles. This database is available on CD-ROM and is used to find articles that have been published in psychological journals.

Read.Me File   File that is included with any program that you download from the Internet and holds the instructions on how to install and run the program.

Root Menu   Menu that you will go into when you access your Gopher client.

Signoff   To stop receiving e-mail from an e-mail discussion group.

Site   Particular place on the Internet such as a WWW page or FTP address.

SLIP Connection   Special connection to the Internet that allows you to use graphical WWW browsers.

Smiley   :) special character that is used on the Internet to indicate that the writer is happy.

Subdirectory   Directory inside a directory that is used to keep computer files separated by category.

Subject Line   First line in an e-mail that the user sees before the e-mail is opened that will let the reader know what the e-mail is about.

Surf   To explore and search the Internet with or without a goal in mind. It is often done just for fun.

System Prompt   Your account directory.

Systems Operator   Person (also called a sysop) in charge of running the computer system where your Internet account is located. The sysop will know all the information you will need to know to get started on the Internet.

Text Browser   WWW browser that allows you to view text only.

Text Editor   Computer program that is used to edit text files.

Text Files   Computer files that consist of text only as opposed to program files.

Thread   Discussion on a newsgroup that consists of a posting and several responses.

Universal Resource Locator   Also known as URLs. The address that you use to access a site using a Web browser.

UNIX™   Disk operating system that is used on many computers connected to the Internet.

Upload   To copy a file from your computer or floppy disk to a computer on the Internet.

URL   Universal Resource Locator. Address of a Gopher or WWW site.

Usenet Newsgroups   Electronic bulletin boards where individuals can post and download text, sounds, and pictures.

User   Person that uses a computer.

Virus   Computer programs that copy themselves onto other computers or floppy disks and are usually designed to damage the computer or disk in some way.

Virus Protection Program   Program that is designed to scan your hard drive and floppy disks for viruses. These programs are available from software distributors and as shareware on the Internet.

Web Page   Site on the World Wide Web.

World Wide Web   Also known as WWW or Web. The most advanced program on the Internet that allows you to access text, software, sounds, and pictures without having to download them.

X-Modem   Downloading protocol.

Y-Modem   Downloading protocol.